EXPERIMENTAL
ORGANIC
CHEMISTRY

A SYNTHETIC & MECHANISTIC PERSPECTIVE

Ralph Nicholas Salvatore

Kyung Woon Jung

University of South Florida

HOUGHTON MIFFLIN COMPANY   Boston   New York

Custom Publishing Editor: Kyle Henderson
Custom Publishing Production Manager: Kathleen McCourt

This work was produced by Houghton Mifflin Custom Publishing and contains material not subject to Houghton Mifflin Company editorial review. The author is responsible for editing, accuracy, and content.

Cover Designer: Joel Gendron
Cover Photograph: PhotoDisc, Inc.

Printed in the United States of America.

ISBN: 0-618-19885-7
N00499

7 8 9 – CCI – 04

Houghton Mifflin
Custom Publishing

222 Berkeley Street • Boston, MA 02116

Address all correspondence and order information to the above address.

Acknowledgements

The authors would like to thank Mr. Vincent L. Flanders for spending invaluable hours of hard work and dedication in helping to type and proofread this laboratory manual, as well as advising on students perspectives.

The authors wish to acknowledge Mr. John Seals and the stockroom staff for their helpful comments and suggestions. We also desire to express great appreciation for all the years' efforts of Professor George R. Wenzinger and Professor George R. Jurch, Jr. in the organic chemistry laboratories at the University of South Florida. Also, we wish to gratefully acknowledge Professor Leon Mandell for his support and his valuable years teaching organic chemistry.

Finally, we dedicate this book to our family and special friends whom we wish to thank for their encouragement, support, and patience.

Contents

- Esterification-Synthesis of Methyl Benzoate
- Nitration of Methyl Benzoate
- Friedel-Crafts Acylation of Ferrocene
- Preparation of a 2,4-Dinitrophenylhydrazone Derivative of an Unknown Aldehyde or Ketone
- Grignard Synthesis of Triphenylmethanol
- Wittig Reaction-Synthesis of *trans*-9-(2-phenylethenyl)anthracene
- Synthesis of Dibenzalacetone by the Aldol Condensation
- Enzymatic Reactions-Enzymatic Reduction of a Ketone to a Chiral Alcohol

Chapter 1

General Guidelines for
Organic Chemistry Laboratories
I & II

Post-Lab Report

It is strongly encouraged that one should try to make all reports written reasonably and scientifically. No emotional essays will be accepted.

I. Introduction

State briefly the purpose of the experiment that you performed.

II. Theoretical Background

With use of any organic textbooks or referenced books, one should include any necessary theoretical background such as reaction mechanisms and physical properties. Point out only salient features (*i.e.,* side reactions), which one should be concerned about in an effort to obtain the best experimental result.

III. Data & Results

Re-organize the raw data and post it in the report.

IV. Discussion

You should evaluate your data and results, and make comments on how good and how bad they were. Explain the reasons and causes of the results, and how one can seek a better protocol based on appropriate approaches, encompassing logical rationale and theoretical background. Any supporting evidence or precedents should be mentioned in your own style and the references that you use should be cited in the References section. Any reasonable discussion is welcome, for example, better experimental design and applications.

V. References

The aforementioned sections should be based on known knowledge or your own reasoning. If you adopt any material from books and journals, you should cite them therein appropriately. Information obtained from the internet must be cited as well.

Lab Reports

Each of the experiments performed will involve the write-up of a formal report. It should present your results and conclusions clearly in an organized fashion with the purpose of convincing the reader you have achieved and understood the goal of each experiment. Its success will depend partly on the quality of the information obtained, and largely on the organization and interpretation of the information. A narrative or writing of your "memoirs" will not be acceptable. The report should be neat, concise, and clearly convey your point. Some comments on a suitable organization of your report are discussed below.

- All laboratory reports should be written neatly in blue or black ink. Typing is also acceptable. If a mistake is made, the incorrect entry should have one line drawn through it. Do not scribble over incorrect entries. White out should never be used in scientific reports.

- All portions of the lab report should be labeled clearly. For example: Introduction, Results, Discussion, etc. Refer to the post-lab report guidelines for appropriate sections.

- The results of the experiment should be clearly and concisely discussed. Focus on interpretation, rather than a rambling plot approach. The report should include a certain amount of scientific information deemed relevant. However, a report with large amount of writing <u>does not</u> guarantee a good grade. Organization of raw data in table form may help.

- Mechanistic interpretation of each organic reaction should be discussed in the report. You should push the arrows in the proper fashion. Consult the literature for help with this.

- Any possible side reactions that may occur during the experiment should be discussed and shown through realistic equations.

- Keep in mind the following points to include when organizing your report: Did you identify the compound if it was an unknown? Summarize the evidence of the identity. Evidence of purity and physical properties, including literature references. Spectroscopic properties and interpretation, including literature references. Chemical behavior and interpretation, including chemical equations. Properties of the derivative if one was made, including literature references.

- You should properly reference all literature used for each experiment in the proper fashion. If textbooks are used, you should cite them accordingly with the author's name, title, publisher, and year. If the world wide web is used, provide the appropriate web address.

Laboratory Notebook

- Use a bound notebook preferably pre-numbered by the manufacturer. A notebook containing removable duplicate pages with carbon copies is optional. No particular format for writing in the lab notebook will be required. However, keep the following points in mind:

- Each page should include a date, and a title of the experiment performed.

- You should record all data and observations while the experiment is in progress. Pre-lab write-ups which should include an experimental procedure, chemical and physical data on chemicals used, preliminary data, such as chemical structures, chemical reactions, hazardous and toxicity data, etc. should all be written before the lab. For properties of chemicals, see The Merck Index, Sigma or Aldrich Catalogue, CRC Handbook, etc.

- Data and observations should not be changed unless an error is made or a step is repeated. The original value should be crossed out legibly and rewritten.

- Balanced chemical equations, principal side reactions, and mechanisms of organic reactions will be included in the formal report. You do not have to include them in your notebook. For mechanistic information, see any standard Organic Chemistry Laboratory Textbooks.

• Draw conclusions from the observations made. This part, of course, can be written after leaving the laboratory. This includes percent yields. See the sample calculation.

Sample Percent Yield Calculation

A **percent yield** is simply the percent of the theoretical amount of product obtained in a reaction. You must be familiar with this calculation for all synthetic reactions in this course.

$$\% \text{ yield} = \frac{\text{actual}}{\text{theoretical}} \times 100$$

EXAMPLE: In the following synthesis, 1.0 g of glycine was acetylated using 2.5 g of acetic anhydride. At the end of the experiment, 1.38 g of acetylglycine had been isolated. Calculate the percent yield of acetylglycine obtained from the following reaction.

1) Calculate all molecular weights.

2) Calculate the number of moles of each reagent involved in the reaction. Do not consider catalytic amounts of reagents or solvent.

	Glycine	Acetic Anhydride	Acetylglycine
MW:	75.1 g/mol	102 g/mol	117 g/mol
weight:	1.0 g	2.5 g	?
moles:	0.0133	0.0245	?

3) Determine the **limiting reagent** (the reagent present in the least amount). This information comes from the balanced chemical equation. This equation is balanced as it stands, so the stoichiometry of the reactants is 1:1. Therefore, in this particular reaction, glycine is the limiting reagent, while the acetic acid is present in excess.

4) Determine the theoretical number of moles of product possible. In this case, 0.0133 mole of glycine is the maximum yield. This value is the same as the limiting reagent value in moles.

5) Convert the theoretical yield to grams.

0.0133 mole of glycine x 117 g/mol =1.56 g (theoretical yield)

6) Use the percent yield equation above.

(1.38 g/1.56 g) x 100 = 88%

LABORATORY SAFETY RULES

EYE PROTECTION: Splash goggles (American Optical 4848, Cesco 522-C, or departmentally approved equivalent) must be worn over the eyes at all time in the laboratory, regardless of what is being done. Contact lenses should not be worn during the lab period.

FOOTWEAR: Shoes must be worn at all times during the laboratory. The feet must be adequately covered (the foot must be totally covered up to the ankle). Therefore sandals and open-toed shoes are not acceptable.

CLOTHING: Clothing must be worn which covers the same parts of the body that are covered by a short sleeve full length lab coat (coverage must be <u>down</u> below the knee and down the arm to a point halfway from the shoulder to the elbow). Therefore, tank tops, halters, shorts, cutoffs, etc. are not acceptable. Lab coats and aprons may be worn but will not be accepted as a substitute for proper clothing.

HAIR: If hair is long enough to interfere with the experiment, it must be tied back.

FOOD: Eating or drinking in the laboratories is prohibited.

SMOKING: Smoking in or near the laboratories is prohibited at all times.

OPEN FLAMES: Open flames of any type are prohibited in the laboratory, unless specific permission is granted to use them.

SCHEDULE: Students will work only during their scheduled laboratory period and never alone or unsupervised.

EMERGENCY EQUIPMENT: Know the location and use of all safety equipment and exits.

CHEMICALS: A) Never taste any chemical B) Never pipet with your mouth C) If you spill chemicals on your hands or body, immediately flush liberally with water. Get further directions from your instructor D) Use chemicals that generate harmful vapors in the hood only E) Return reagent bottles to their place after using. Never pour unused chemicals back into reagent bottles.

WASTE DISPOSAL: Chemicals and used materials should be discarded in specified containers. When in doubt check with your instructor.

ACCIDENTS: Report all accidents however minor to your instructor immediately.

WORK SPACE: Keep your working space neat at all times and clean up when you leave for the day. Return equipment to its proper place.

Chapter 2

Organic Chemistry Laboratory I Experiments

Organic Chemistry Laboratory I Syllabus

This course is designed to provide students with the fundamental techniques of organic chemistry including methods of isolation, purification, and structural identification with applications to synthetic and mechanistic problems. This course will focus on fundamental reactions and techniques applicable to various fields of organic chemistry. Students are advised to understand, prior to coming to lab, what they will perform in practice, and they are also strongly encouraged to use a problem solving approach during the class as well as while writing post lab reports. Scientific organization and writing will be other goals of this course.

Schedule of Experiments

Lab Meeting # 1   Check-in and Safety lecture.

Lab Meeting # 2   Exp. 1: Simple and Fractional Distillation of a Binary Mixture.

Lab Meeting # 3   Exp. 2: Acid-Base Extraction: Separation of an Organic Acid, a Base, and a Neutral Substance.

Lab Meeting # 4   Exp. 3: Chromatography-Identification of the Composition of an Unknown Analgesic Tablet and Isolation of β-Carotene from Spinach Leaves.

Lab Meeting # 5   Exp. 4: Chirality-Isolation of Limonene from Citrus Fruits.

Lab Meeting # 6   Exp. 5: Isolation of Trimyristin from Nutmeg.

Lab Meeting # 7   Exp. 6: Preparation of Myristic Acid from Trimyristin by Hydrolysis.

Lab Meeting # 8	Exp. 7: Synthesis and Reactivity of *tert*-Butyl Chloride Via an S_n1 Reaction.
Lab Meeting # 9	Exp. 8: Bromination: Synthesis of 1-Bromobutane from 1-Butanol.
Lab Meeting # 10	Exp. 9: Alkenes from Alcohols: Analysis of a Mixture by Gas Chromatography.
Lab Meeting # 11	Exp. 10: Alkene Addition Reactions: Organic Qualitative Chemical Analysis of Unsaturation.
Lab Meeting # 12	Exp. 11: Spectroscopy: Infrared and Nuclear Magnetic Resonance Spectroscopy.
Lab Meeting # 13	*Make-up Lab.*
Lab Meeting # 14	Check-out and Clean up.

Experiment 1: Simple and Fractional Distillation of a Binary Mixture

I) *Aim of the Experiment*

In this experiment you will perform simple and fractional distillation in order to separate a mixture of two liquids, namely cyclohexane and toluene.

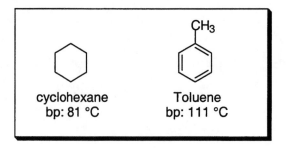

cyclohexane
bp: 81 °C

Toluene
bp: 111 °C

II) *Introduction*

Distillation is the process in which a liquid is vaporized, the vapor is condensed by cooling it, and the condensate or distillate is collected. This method of purification is extremely useful for separating a liquid mixture based on boiling point differences.

liquid $\underset{\text{Condensation}}{\overset{\text{Evaporation}}{\rightleftharpoons}}$ Vapor

The **boiling point** of a liquid is defined as the temperature at which its vapor pressure equals atmospheric pressure. The boiling point is a physical characteristic that can be used as important evidence to a liquid's identity as well as its purity.

Distillation techniques are often used to separate two or more components on the basis of their vapor pressures. Vapor pressure results from molecules in motion as they leave the liquid surface and become vapor. Separation is usually then accomplished by taking advantage of the fact that the component with a higher vapor pressure, lower boiling point, will be in higher concentration in the vapor phase. Therefore, the lower boiling liquid will be collected first.

There are two distillation techniques you need to be familiar with in the organic chemistry lab. **Simple distillation** works well for most routine separations and purification of organic compounds when the boiling points of the two components are large. However, when the boiling point difference of the components is small, **fractional distillation** makes use of a **fractionating column** which allows for repeated vaporizations and condensations, thus providing a better separation of a liquid mixture.

III) Experimental Procedure

A) Simple Distillation of a Mixture of Cyclohexane and Toluene.

Place 6 mL of the stock solution containing a mixture of cyclohexane and toluene (1:1) into a 10 mL conical vial and add a boiling stone. Set up the apparatus for simple distillation as seen on the course web page and use a graduated conical vial for the receiver. Clamp the apparatus firmly in place. Bury the vial deep in the sand bath so that the liquid in the vial is below the surface of the sand. Position the hot plate beneath the sand bath. *Carefully*, align the top of the thermometer bulb below the side arm of the distillation head. *Note*: It is crucial that the thermometer be positioned in the appropriate location for accurate boiling point measurements. Using another thermometer, position it completely in the sand bath, so you can monitor the bath temperature. Before beginning the distillation, be sure that you can remove the distillate as it collects without disturbing the distillation. Also, have your instructor check your set-up. Initiate the distillation and heat at a reasonable rate. Once the liquid in the vial begins to boil, reduce the heating rate to ~2-3 °C per minute to allow for proper establishment of equilibrium between the liquid and vapor phases. *If you heat the vial too quickly, both liquids will distill over together, resulting in <u>no</u> separation. The rate of distillation should be no faster than two drops per minute!*

> *Monitor the distillation rate appropriately, and make adjustments accordingly. Do not let the temperature rise too rapidly.*

As the distillation progresses, you will note a ring of liquid moving up the vial into the distillation head. The temperature should rise as well at this point, and you should observe the walls of the setup become wet as the vapor condenses. Continue a *slow, steady heating* until the temperature of the inside thermometer rises rapidly and then reaches a more or less steady value (~80 °C). Then, conduct the distillation, collecting the major fraction without *interruption. Note and record the temperature range and volume of distillate for the fraction collected at regular time intervals.* Record the volume of the distillate by reading the graduations on the vial. Make estimations if necessary. When the first fraction has more or less completely distilled (~3 ml), you will notice that the temperature will either decrease or begin to increase. At this point, change to a new graduated conical vial. Store the steady boiling fraction in a screw-capped vial and label it fraction # 1 after collection is complete. At this point, turn up the hot plate to distill the higher boiling component (toluene), and collect the second steady boiling fraction (~110 °C) as before. Insulation may be necessary. Continue the distillation until the second component is nearly all collected. *Note and record the temperature range and volume of distillate for this fraction collected as well.* Store the second fraction in screw-capped vial and label it as fraction # 2. **However, never distill to dryness!**

Discontinue the distillation, and shut off the hot plate. Allow the apparatus to cool, and disassemble. Graph a distillation curve of your results on graph paper neatly. Label the y-axis as temperature and the x-axis as volume of distillate. Be sure equal spacing is used for both axes accordingly.

B) Fractional Distillation of a Mixture of Cyclohexane and Toluene.

In a 10 mL vial, place 6 ml of the stock solution of cyclohexane and toluene, then add a boiling stone. Set up the apparatus as in simple distillation, however, insert the small fractionating column containing aluminum mesh packing chips, between the vial and the distillation head (See course web page). TWO OR THREE ALUMINUM MESH CHIPS ARE SUFFICIENT FOR THIS DISTILLATION. More packing material will hold back the higher boiling material to be distilled, causing column overload. The packing will allow for efficient separation of cyclohexane and toluene. Insulate the column by wrapping with aluminum foil to keep the temperature of the column constant. Use a 5 mL graduated conical vial for collecting the distillate. Assemble the thermometer as above, and mount the apparatus in a sand bath using a clamp. Bury the vial deep in the sand for efficient heating. Again heat steadily, using a hot plate. *Do not allow the temperature to rise too rapidly, and distill the mixture at a rate of no faster than two drops per minute!*

Once constant but gentle boiling begins, lower the heating rate and heat slowly at a constant rate to permit a good separation. Record the temperature and volume at regular increments in your notebook. Remove what you regard to be the pure cyclohexane fraction as previously done in simple distillation and store the liquid in a numbered screw-capped vial. After you have distilled off the cyclohexane, change the receiver to another 5 mL graduated conical vial and turn the hot plate up and collect the toluene as done previously above. Record temperature and volumes accordingly at regular intervals.

Discontinue the distillation. Allow the apparatus to cool and disassemble the distillation set up. Graph your results in the same fashion as above.

Interpret and explain your results in your report. Include an appropriate discussion of the difference between the two graphs. A sample of each graph is illustrated below.

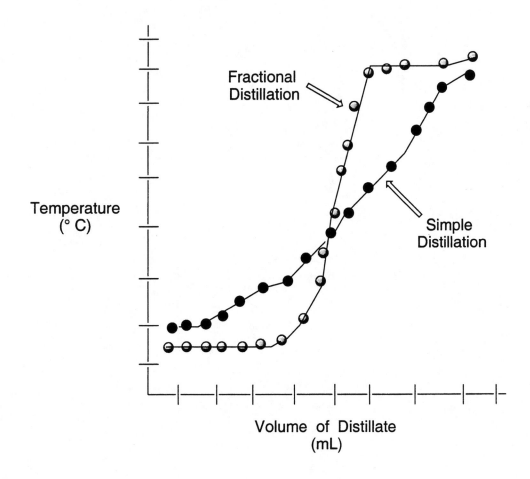

IV) Post-Lab Report

Include the following points in the theoretical background section of your Post-Lab Report:
• Boiling point of a liquid and vapor pressure.
• Distillation: Simple vs. Fractional.

• Raoult's, Daltons Law, and Mole fraction.

•Azeotrope.

• Theoretical plates.

• In the Discussion section of your report, evaluate your own results accordingly to the points described above. Also, discuss the problems and concerns, which commonly arise in distillations, and explain their causes. Suggest reasonable solutions and alternative methods if appropriate.

Experiment 2: Acid-Base Extraction: Separation of an Organic Acid, a Base, and a Neutral Compound

I) Aim of the Experiment

The purpose of the experiment is to carry out an acid-base extraction in order to separate a mixture of benzoic acid, 4-chloroaniline and naphthalene, and characterize each by melting point.

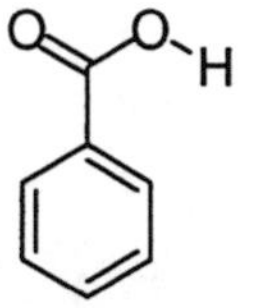

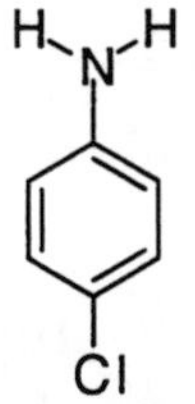

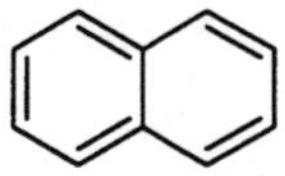

Benzoic acid
mp 122 °C

(a carboxylic acid)
an **Acid**

4-Chloroaniline
mp 68-71°C

(an amine)
a **Base**

Naphthalene
mp 80 °C

(an aromatic hydrocarbon)
a **Neutral compound**

II) Introduction

Along with distillation and recrystallization, extraction is one of the most useful separation techniques in organic chemistry. Organic reactions sometimes result in a mixture of products, by-products, and starting materials, some of which can differ significantly from the others in the way the distribute themselves between two immiscible solvents. The idea behind extraction is to use two liquids, one being an organic solvent and the other an aqueous phase, so that the desired product dissolves in one while undesired by-products or starting materials dissolve in the other. Since the two liquids are immiscible, they will form two layers and are easily separated by drawing off the lower layer by a standard piece of lab equipment known as a **separatory funnel**. **Extraction** provides a means of "pulling" the desired compound out of one phase into another by shaking the solution with a different solvent.

There are several key points to keep in mind during an extraction. One is always to be aware of which layer is the organic phase and which is the aqueous phase. The more dense liquid or solution will of course always be on the bottom. If you are ever in doubt about which layer is which, remove a drop of the layer and add it to a small test tube containing water. If it becomes homogeneous (or miscible), it is aqueous; if not it is organic. How much of the compound or solute dissolves in each phase depend on the solubility of the solute in each solvent. The ratio of the concentrations of the solute in each solvent at a particular temperature is a constant called the **distribution coefficient** or the **partition coefficient** (*K*).

$$K = \frac{\text{concentration in solvent}_2}{\text{concentration in solvent}_1}$$

where solvent$_1$ and solvent$_2$ are immiscible liquids

Secondly, save all discarded layers until the final product is in hand. It would be wise to label each as well. This precaution is taken so that if by chance you save the wrong layer, your product can be recovered.

The key to separating organic compounds by an acid-base extraction consists of the choice of extraction solvent, and on the acidic or basic properties among the starting materials or products.

The solvent used in the extraction should have many important properties. It should have a high solubility for the organic compound; be immiscible with the other solvent (usually water); it should have a relatively low boiling point so that the solvent can easily be removed from the compound after extraction; it should be nontoxic, non-reactive, readily available and inexpensive.

The solubility properties of these organic acids and bases and their salt forms allows us to separate these materials from each other as well as from neutral organic molecules. An acid compound will react with base to form a salt. For example a strong organic acid, *i.e.,* benzoic acid, will react with an inorganic base (sodium hydroxide, a strong base) to form the salt, sodium benzoate which immediately dissolves in the aqueous layer, leaving the basic compound and the neutral compound in the organic layer. After the layers are separated, the benzoic acid can be regenerated by treating the aqueous layer with acid (*i.e.,* aqueous hydrochloric acid). The basic compound can then be separated in a similar fashion. This reactive property provides the basis of acid-base extraction. Below is a flow diagram for the separation of a generic carboxylic acid, an amine, and a neutral compound.

III) Experimental Procedure

Place 3 g of a stock mixture containing benzoic acid, 4-chloroaniline and naphthalene (all of equal weights) in a 125 mL Erlenmeyer flask. Add 30 mL of diethyl ether, and transfer the mixture to a 125 mL separatory funnel using a little fresh ether to complete the transfer (~20 mL). Add 30 mL of 5 % HCl and stopper the funnel. Immediately invert the funnel over, holding the stopper in place, and vent the funnel. Be sure not to point it at anyone. *Exercise care when handling diethyl ether since it is known to be an anesthetic if inhaled in large quantities. Also, avoid contact with the skin and clothing when using 5 % HCl.* Shake the mixture vigorously with frequent venting of the funnel. Be sure you do not allow pressure to build up in the funnel, since diethyl ether is a volatile organic solvent. Allow the layers to separate completely, and then place the separatory funnel in an iron ring supported on ring stand at your bench top. Draw off the lower layer into a 125 mL Erlenmeyer flask (labeled flask # 1). Be sure to remove the stopper before draining the separatory funnel. This layer now contains the protonated

11

amine, while the ether layer (top), contains the benzoic acid and naphthalene. Place the separatory funnel back in the iron ring and place the stopper in place.

Carefully, make basic the acid extract in flask #1 by cooling in an ice bath and adding 3 M NaOH dropwise, checking with pH paper to be sure that the solution is basic. To test the pH, dip a glass rod into the solution and touch a strip of pH paper. The free base (4-chloroaniline) should precipitate out. Cool the flask in ice, and allow to stand for ten-fifteen minutes. Once precipitate fully has formed, collect the solid by vacuum filtration. Rinse the product with small portions of cold ice water, scrape the dry crystal out of the buchner funnel and press them dry between two pieces of filter paper. Allow the product to air dry, and proceed with the rest of the experiment.

To the original ether solution still in the separatory funnel, add 50 mL of 5 % NaOH. *Exercise care when handeling base as well.* Stopper it, vent it, and then shake it several times with frequent venting. Remove the stopper, draw off the aqueous layer into an Erlenmeyer flask and label as # 2. *Cautiously*, acidify the contents of flask # 2 by dropwise addition of 6 M HCl, while cooling in an ice bath. Check if the contents are acidic, once again using pH paper. Collect the precipitate (benzoic acid) by vacuum filtration, and wash with ice water as done previously above. Dry the product as above and allow to air dry until the end of the experiment.

At this point, the neutral compound (naphthalene) should still be in the ether layer. Add 20 mL of saturated sodium chloride solution to the separatory funnel to remove any residual water present, extract as above, and discard the bottom aqueous layer. Drain the ether layer into a 125 ml Erlenmeyer flask (label flask # 3) and add enough anhydrous sodium sulfate to dry the organic layer. Allow to stand for several minutes. Decant or filter the drying agent into a tared 125 mLvacuum flask, rinse the drying agent with fresh diethyl ether (10- 15 mL), and add it to the vacuum flask. Evaporate the ether using an aspirator (use a trap!) until a solid remains. Use the steam bath to aid this process. Determine the weight of the dry crude naphthalene. Take each product's melting point. Compare each product's melting point to the literature value and comment on the purity of each in your post-lab report.

IV) Post-Lab Report

In your Post-Lab report, discuss the following points in your theoretical background section:
• Acid-Base Extraction: purpose, theory, and technique.
• Distribution or Partition Coefficient.

• Think and comment on the difference and efficiency with regard to the following comparison: Using less volume of solvent (2 mL), and extracting more times (5 times), vs. using more volume (5 mL) and extracting less number of times (2 times).

• Melting point: Identity (comparison to the literature value) and product purity (melting point range). NO DISCUSSION OF MELTING POINT THEORY IS NEEDED HERE, AS IT WILL BE COVERED IN EXPERIMENT-5. HOWEVER, YOU WILL HAVE TO DICUSS AND COMPARE THE DATA AND RESULTS IN THIS EXPERIMENT ONCE AGAIN TO THOSE OBTAINED IN EXPERIMENT 5. INTERPRET AND COMPARE THE DIFFERENCE.

• Include any problems one might encounter in this experiment, and how one may suggest alternative methods to solve such problems.

Experiment 3: Chromatography: Identification of the Composition of an Unknown Analgesic Tablet by TLC

I) Aim of the Experiment

The purpose of this experiment is to analyze several analgesics by thin layer chromatography (TLC) and to identify the composition of an unknown tablet.

Acetaminophen   Aspirin   Caffeine   Ibuprofen

II) Introduction

Chromatography is a method of separating compounds and the term originates from the first example, in which colored substances were separated. However, chromatography is not only limited to separating colored compounds. Three types of chromatography are used extensively in organic chemistry and will be used in the course. *"Thin layer chromatography"* (TLC), *"gas liquid chromatography"* (GC), and *"column chromatography"*.

Every type of chromatographic analysis depends on a distribution between two phases: a **mobile phase** and a **stationary phase**. The mobile phase consists of a liquid or a gas, which carries the sample through the solid, or liquid, that forms the stationary phase (the adsorbent). The mixture is applied to the adsorbent; the solvent is passed over the surface and some of the compounds adhere strongly to the adsorbent and others move with the solvent.

The adsorbent and the solvent compete for the compounds. The success of the separation depends on the different polarities of the 3 components; (A) the adsorbent (B) the compounds, and (C) the solvent.

The adsorbent is always the most polar compound; some common adsorbents are silica gel and alumina. The compounds in the mixture differ in polarities based on the structure of the compound or functional groups. Solvents also differ in polarities. Depending on the polarities of your compound, one should choose an appropriate solvent for a satisfactory separation.

Thin Layer Chromatography (or TLC) is a highly sensitive analytical technique used to gain information about the purity and identity from a very small amount of sample. Generally, although not limited, you will use a plastic plate coated with a thin layer of silica (the adsorbent). A small amount of the mixture to be separated is applied near one end of the plate. The plate is placed in a closed chamber containing a solvent. The solvent rises through the stationary phase by capillary action. As the solvent ascends the plate, the compounds are distributed between the mobile phase and stationary phase. The more the compound binds to the adsorbent, the slower it will move up the plate, and therefore more polar.

TLC can show, by separation of components, how many compounds are present in a mixture. TLC also shows important characteristics such as the polarity of the compound and can be used to identify an unknown.

We will use TLC here in this experiment to determine which common over-the-counter drugs contain which analgesics. Analgesics are commonly known as substances that relieve pain.

III) Experimental Procedure: TLC

Obtain silica plates with fluorescent indicator from the stockroom. Using a **pencil**, about 1 cm from the end of the plate draw a line. Be careful not to touch the rough side of the plate with your fingers. Hold the plate by the edges. Using a micropipet, spot aspirin, acetaminophen, ibuprofen and caffeine, which are available as reference standards. Spot the ibuprofen several times. Use a fresh micropipet for each. *Exert care not to overspot each standard.* Examine the plate under UV light to see if the compound was applied, if not, add more. **DO NOT** look directly into the UV lamp. UV light can damage your eyes!

Obtain a chromatography chamber, place a piece of filter paper along the sides and add a mixture of 95% ethyl acetate and 5% acetic acid. These chambers should already be prepared for you. Using tweezers, place the plate you spotted vertically in the chamber against the filter paper. When the solvent front has moved to about 1/2 cm from the top edge, remove the plate, and draw a line for the solvent front using a pencil. After the plate has dried, examine the plate under UV light and using a pencil, outline the spots. Note the color of the spots and record. Place the plate in an iodine chamber and let it remain for about 2 minutes. *Do not breathe or get iodine on your skin.* Record the information and calculate the R_f value for each. Use the equation below. An example of a typical TLC result is also shown.

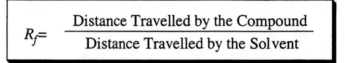

$$R_f = \frac{\text{Distance Travelled by the Compound}}{\text{Distance Travelled by the Solvent}}$$

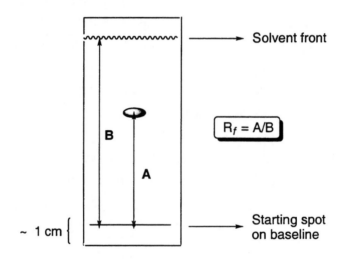

On another TLC plate, draw the base line mark and label the four standards. Apply the standards to the plate. Obtain an unknown tablet already crushed from your instructor. Add this to a small test tube or vial and add some ethanol, and mix. Not all the tablet will dissolve, but enough will go into solution to spot the plate. Apply the unknown as the fifth spot to the plate, develop and visualize as noted before. Identify the unknown composition and calculate its R_f value. Note colors seen under UV light and iodine stain in your notebook.

Chromatography: Column Chromatography-Isolation of β-Carotene from Spinach Leaves

IV) Aim of the Experiment

In this experiment, you will use the technique of column chromatography to separate ß-carotene from a mixture of many plant pigments found in spinach.

β-carotene

V) Introduction

Column chromatography is similar to TLC in principle, but done on a larger scale. It can be primarily used to **separate** and **isolate** compounds rather than analyze a mixture.

ß-Carotene is the least polar of all plant pigments that are found in spinach leaves. It is a bright yellow-orange pigment commonly found in carrots. ß-carotene possesses 11 conjugated double bonds and the chain ends possess 2 rings.

This experiment consists of several parts:
- Preparation of a micro-column.
- Extraction of pigment mixture from spinach leaves.
- Isolation of ß-carotene by column chromatography.
- TLC of extracted and purified products.

VI) Experimental Procedure: Column chromatography

Obtain a micro-column from the stockroom. Fill the column approximately half way with silica gel, and pack the silica gel by tapping the column with your hands or a piece of rubber tubing. Add ~1/2 cm of sand on top of the silica gel. Clamp the column vertically on your bench using a small clamp.

Obtain some frozen chopped spinach that has been defrosted. Weigh out approximately 2 g and transfer it to a small Erlenmeyer flask. Add 15 mL of ethyl acetate and, using a spatula, *mash* the spinach for several minutes. Pipet or decant the solution into another Erlenmeyer flask. Dry using anhydrous sodium sulfate. Decant the solution into a 125 mL vacuum flask and remove the solvent using an aspirator over the steam bath. Use an aspirator trap. Add a boiling stick to prevent bumping.

Dissolve the residue in ~5-6 drops of 1:1 ethyl acetate–petroleum ether solution. Reserve a drop or two for TLC in a capped vial.

Obtain 15 mL of petroleum ether from the stockroom. Pre-number 6 small test tubes and place them in a test tube rack. Wet the column with petroleum ether and allow it to drip through. Use a gentle stream of air to force the solvent through quicker. This procedure is known as **flash column chromatography**. Add the spinach residue to the wet column. Let it run down onto the sand. Add a few more drops of petroleum ether to the flask and transfer to the column. Repeat this wash step. Allow the solution to run down the sand and fill the column with petroleum ether. Begin to run the column (use air) and collect the fractions in the test tubes. Keep the column running until the first colored material elutes. You may wish to collect other colored fractions, but you will be unable to characterize their identity. Record in your notebook the approximate volume and colors of solutions in the test tubes. When the experiment is complete, discard the silica gel from the column into the hazardous waste.

Transfer the same colored fractions to a 50 mL Erlenmeyer flask and evaporate the solvent using an aspirator. Again, use heat from the steam bath if necessary. Dissolve the residue in 3 drops of hexane and TLC the crude and purified mixture against standard ß-carotene. Use hexane for the chamber solvent. Spot your pure compound after evaporation approximately 15 times, since this compound is dilute. The pure ß-carotene will be highly concentrated. Determine whether you were successful at isolating and purifying ß-carotene, by visualizing both by UV light and I_2.

VII) Post-Lab Report:

In your Post-Lab report, include the following points:
• Brief discussion of the theory behind chromatography: why is it used? What information one can obtain from it etc. Include points such as the difference between mobile and

stationary phase, affinity, the adsorbent, polarity of molecules relative to elution order, solvent polarity, R_f value, etc.

• The difference and similarities between TLC and column chromatography.

• Clearly discuss how you determined the identity of your unknown tablet in the TLC experiment. Use R_f values as compared to the authentic samples and visualization techniques. BE SURE TO RELATE THE FOUR MOLECULE'S RELATIVE POLARITIES TO R_f VALUES AND FUNCTIONAL GROUPS PRESENT.

• Discuss if your column separation was successful and how you determined this.

• Include any problems one might encounter in both parts of these experiments, and how one may suggest alternatives to solve these problems.

Experiment 4:Chirality-Isolation of Limonene from Citrus Fruits

I) Aim of the Experiment

The purpose of this experiment is to extract the essential oil, limonene, from the peels of a variety of citrus fruit and analyze it by polarimetry.

II) Introduction

Essential oils make up a large group of organic compounds obtained from plants. These oils are often characterized by very distinct odors, and are dependent on a certain degree of stereochemistry found in the particular molecule. Many of these essential oils belong to a class of compounds called **terpenes**. Terpenes are compounds made up of two or more five carbon units, named isoprene.

Limonene is a terpene that can be isolated from orange peels almost 100% in the (R)-(+)-limonene form. Other citrus fruits such as lemons, limes, grapefruits, and tangerines contain this natural product as well. The purity of this oil can be determined easily by measuring its physical properties including optical rotation by use of a polarimeter.

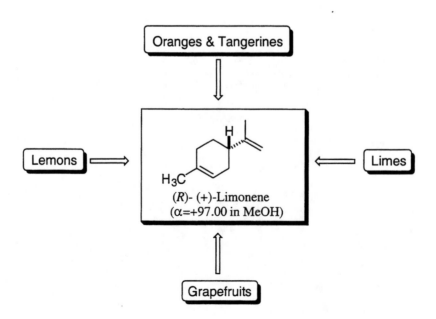

The natural product limonene in this experiment will be isolated by technique known as steam distillation. **Steam distillation** is the distillation of a mixture of water (steam) and an organic compound or a mixture of organic compounds. The organic compounds must be insoluble in water for the steam distillation to be successful. Immiscible mixtures such as water and an organic compound do not behave like solutions. The components of the immiscible mixture boil at lower temperatures than the boiling points of any of the components. Natural products, such as flavorings and perfumes found in leaves and flowers, are sometimes separated from their sources using this method.

III) Experimental Procedure

Peel the same citrus fruit for this experiment. Your instructor will give you details on which fruit to use. Use 3/4 of a grapefruit, 1 orange, or 2 lemons or 2 limes. Weigh the peelings. When peeling, remove most of the white pulp and keep the outer portion of the peel. After weighing the peel, grind them into a slurry using a blender. Pour the liquid peel into a 250 mL round bottom flask using a powder funnel and assemble a steam distillation apparatus, as demonstrated by your instructor. Rinse the blender with 120 mL of distilled H_2O and add it to the round bottom flask containing the citrus peels. In this procedure, steam is generated *in situ*. Attach a 50 ml graduated cylinder as a receiver and begin the steam distillation.

Heat the mixture strongly using a heating mantle. During the distillation, monitor and record the temperature of the distillation as well as any odors clearly noticeable. Collect approximately 40 mL of liquid. Do not allow solid material from the pulp to distill over with your liquid. Also, if foaming occurs and starts to distill, let your instructor know. You should notice a small layer of oil floating on top of the surface of the water after the distillation.

Using a 250 mL separatory funnel, extract the distillate three times with 30 mL of dichloromethane. Each time, rinse the flask with a few milliliters of dichloromethane and transfer to the separatory funnel. Shake the funnel and vent frequently. Separate the layers, keeping in mind the density of CH_2Cl_2 and H_2O. Combine all the organic layers in a 250 mL Erlenmeyer flask and dry the solution using anhydrous sodium sulfate for 15 minutes. After that time period, filter the drying agent into a pre-weighed 250 mL filter flask. Rinse the drying agent with a few milliliters of dichloromethane and add it to the flask. Remove the solvent using an aspirator connected to a trap. The remaining liquid in the flask will be crude limonene. Weigh the oil and record this in your notebook. Be sure all solvent is removed at this point. Describe the appearance and odor of the oil in your notebook.

IV) Polarimetry

There are several ways to determine the optical purity of a compound synthesized in the organic laboratory. The simplest involves measuring the optical rotation using an instrument known as a **polarimeter**. It consists of a light source and two prisms. One prism is used to produce plane-polarized light; the other detects the rotation in the plane of polarization. A tube containing a solution of a compound to be analyzed is placed between the two prisms. Finally, there is a viewing device with a scale indicating the angle by which the plane of polarized light has been rotated.

The **optical rotation** of a chiral compound is a specific physical property of the compound, and is determined and reported like melting and boiling points. Different chiral compounds have widely varying specific rotations. The magnitude of the value of optical rotation depends on a few factors: 1) concentration of the solution, 2) the length of the light path through the solution, 3) wavelength of light, 4) solvent nature, and 5) temperature.

A typical optical rotation example: For cholesterol,

$$[\alpha]_D^{23} = -3.15° \text{ (ethanol)}$$

The **specific rotation** $[\alpha]^{T°C}$ can then be calculated using the equation below from the observed rotation reading from the polarimeter.

Specific Rotation $[\alpha]_D$:

$$[\alpha]_D^{T°C} = \frac{\alpha}{(l \cdot c)}$$

α= observed angle of rotation (polarimeter reading)

l= length of light path (1 decimeter)

c= concentration of sample (g/mL)

T°= temperature of measurement in Celsius

D= sodium D line (wavelength)

The results of polarimetric analysis of a stereoisomer are reported in terms of **enantiomeric excess** (or more common, optical purity). Enantiomeric excess (% ee) is calculated using the expression given below.

$$\% \ ee = \frac{[\alpha] \ observed}{[\alpha] \ pure} \times 100\%$$

Your instructor will provide further theory with regards to polarimetry and optical rotation when you are doing this part of the experiment.

V) Experimental Procedure on Polarimetry

With the aid of your instructor, you will determine the optical rotation of your synthesized limonene and compare it to the literature value.

A few points of merit worth mentioning are as follows. First, polarimeters are very expensive and must be handled with care. Be certain no air bubbles or suspended particles are trapped in your prepared solution of limonene. Also, before taking your optical rotation, your instructor will standardize the instrument accordingly using a known compound. MAKE CERTAIN THE INSTRUMENT READING IS ON ZERO BEFORE THE INSTRMENT IS USED !

Dissolve your limonene in 3 mL of 95% ethanol and pipet it into a 10 mL volumetric flask. Rinse the Erlenmeyer flask with several more 1 mL portions of ethanol and transfer to the flask. Fill the volumetric flask to the calibration mark, stopper the flask and invert several times to thoroughly mix! At this point, if your solution is cloudy, you will have to filter it. Consult your instructor if this occurs. Determine the observed rotation of the limonene and record. Calculate the specific rotation $[\alpha]_D$ of your limonene and its enantiomeric excess using the following equations.

VI) Post-Lab Report

Include the following points in your Post-Lab report.

- Steam distillation: theory, technique, purpose, etc.
- Discussion of stereoisomers, laboratory analysis of steroisomers, etc.
- Polarimetry: specific rotation, % ee, what information can be obtained from the values, etc.
- Compare and contrast the yields of limonene and the purity of each obtained from each different type of citrus fruit. Explain and comment on your results as well as the classes data in your report.

Experiment 5: Isolation of Trimyristin from Nutmeg

I) Aim of the Experiment

The purpose of this experiment is to isolate a single compound, trimyristin, from a complex mixture of natural products in its source, nutmeg.

II) Introduction

Trimyristin is a naturally occurring triester that is present in many fats and oils and can be easily isolated from the readily available spice, nutmeg. Since the natural product is in relatively high concentrations in the spice, it can be extracted and isolated in a highly pure form, free from contamination, by closely related esters of glycerol and fatty acids.

Trimyristin
mp 56-58 °C

The natural product will be purified by a technique commonly known in organic chemistry as **recrystallization (or crystallization)**. Recrystallization is the most important method for the purification of solid organic compounds. To carry out a recrystallization, the compound is dissolved in *minimum* amount of hot solvent. The ideal solvent for the recrystallization of a particular compound is one that (1) does not react with the compound; (2) boils at a temperature below the compound's melting point; (3) dissolves a moderately large amount of the compound when hot; (4) dissolves only a small amount of compound when cool; (5) is moderately volatile so that the fine crystals can be dried easily; and (6) is nontoxic, nonflammable, and inexpensive.

If insoluble impurities are present, the hot solution is filtered. If the solution is contaminated with colored impurities, it may be treated with decolorizing charcoal and filtered. The hot, saturated solution is finally allowed to cool *slowly* so that the desired compound crystallizes at a moderate rate. When the crystals are fully formed, they are isolated from the **mother liquor** (the solution) by simple filtration.

Upon successful isolation of trimyristin, the product will be verified by its characteristic melting point. The **melting point** of a crystalline solid is the temperature at which a solid becomes a liquid at normal atmospheric pressure. The melting point of an organic compound in the organic lab typically should be reported as a **melting point range**. A melting point range is determined by slowly heating a small amount of the sample in a **capillary melting point tube** using an instrument known as a **Melt-Temp** apparatus. The temperature at which the first droplet of liquid is observed is the lower temperature of the melting point range and the higher temperature is recorded when the sample is totally in liquid form. Thus, a melting point range might be reported, for example, as 103.5 °-105 °C. Typically, if an organic compound is isolated successfully in pure form, it will have a narrow melting point range (2 degrees or less) and will have a melting point very close when compared to the literature value. If the compound is impure, its melting point will be depressed and its range broadened.

III) Experimental Procedure

A) Isolation of Trimyristin from nutmeg.

Weigh approximately 200 mg of ground nutmeg and transfer it to a 50 mL Erlenmeyer flask. Using a pipet, add 2 mL of diethyl ether and swirl the mixture vigorously for 15 minutes.

During this time, pack a Pasteur pipet with a loose cotton plug (use a boiling stick to push the cotton down), add ~2 mm of sand, and fill with ~1 cm of anhydrous sodium sulfate. Place the pipet through a one-holed rubber septum and clamp it vertically over a pre-weighed 25 mL vacuum flask. Using another clean Pasteur pipet, transfer the contents from the Erlenmeyer flask to the packed Pasteur pipet and allow it to flow into the 10 mL vacuum flask. *Leave undissolved material in the Erlenmeyer flask.* If the flow is too slow or stops, use a rubber bulb and apply slight pressure to the packed pipet. Rinse the packing material with an additional 0.5 mL of ether. Remove the solvent by evaporation using an aspirator connected to a trap. *Caution: Do not use any open flames near diethyl ether, it is extremely flammable!* Exercise care not to get water into the 10 mL vacuum flask. At this point, a solid should be observed, however, if an oil is present, cool the product in an ice bath. Once the product crystallizes, determine the weight of the crude trimyristin and save a very small amount for a melting point. The small amount saved for a crude melting point should be spread out on a watch glass and allowed to air dry until you are ready to take the melting point of the pure product.

B) Purification by Recrystallization.

Add about 0.5 mL of acetone to the crude product and dissolve the residue by gentle heating on the steam bath. Be careful the solution does not over boil! When the solid is in solution, remove the vacuum flask using a test tube holder, and allow it to cool to room temperature. Cover the vacuum flask with a cork. Once cool, place the vial in an ice bath. Collect the solid by suction filtration using a Hirsch funnel (wet the filter paper first with 2 drops of water) and rinse the vial with a small amount of <u>cold</u> acetone. Transfer the solid sample to a pre-weighed vial and obtain the final weight of the pure product. Determine the percent recovery of pure trimyristin from crude trimyristin and from pure nutmeg. Determine the melting point of both the crude and pure trimyristin. Take the melting point slowly! This will allow for a more accurate reading. Record the data in your notebook, compare both melting points and rationalize the difference. Save the dry product for the next lab exercise.

IV) Post-Lab Report:

In your Post-Lab report, discuss the following points:
• Recrystallization: theory, technique, steps, problems, etc.
• Other relevent features to recrystallization: solubility, solute, solvent, temperature.
• Melting point: theory, effects of impurities on the melting point, evidence of product identity and purity, possible errors in technique.
• Discuss clearly if the product, trimyristin, was obtained in pure form from nutmeg, and what evidence you have that illustrates this.
• Discuss comparatively the melting points obtained in Experiment 2.
• Include any problems one might encounter in this experiment, and how one may suggest alternative methods to solve such problems.

Experiment 6: Preparation of Myristic Acid from Trimyristin by Hydrolysis

I) *Aim of the Experiment*

In this experiment, you will synthesize myristic acid from trimyristin by base promoted hydrolysis. The crude myristic acid will be purified by recrystallization and then characterized by melting point.

Myristic acid
mp 54-55 °C

II) *Introduction*

Esters (RCOOR') undergo a common reaction under both acidic and basic conditions known as **hydrolysis**. The products released from the reaction are an alcohol (R'OH) and the anion of the carboxylic acid (RCOOH), as delineated in the reaction below.

Base Hydrolysis of an Ester

Hydrolysis under basic conditions as such is commonly known as **saponification** and is widely used in the manufacturing of commercially available soaps and detergents.

In much the same manner, trimyristin (an ester), by alkaline hydrolysis, will be converted to the sodium salt of myristic acid. Both the salt and glycerol (an alcohol), the other product, are soluble in the reaction solvent. Upon acidification, the myristic acid is easily obtained in solid form as shown below. For every one mole of trimyristin hydrolyzed, 3 moles of myristic acid is produced.

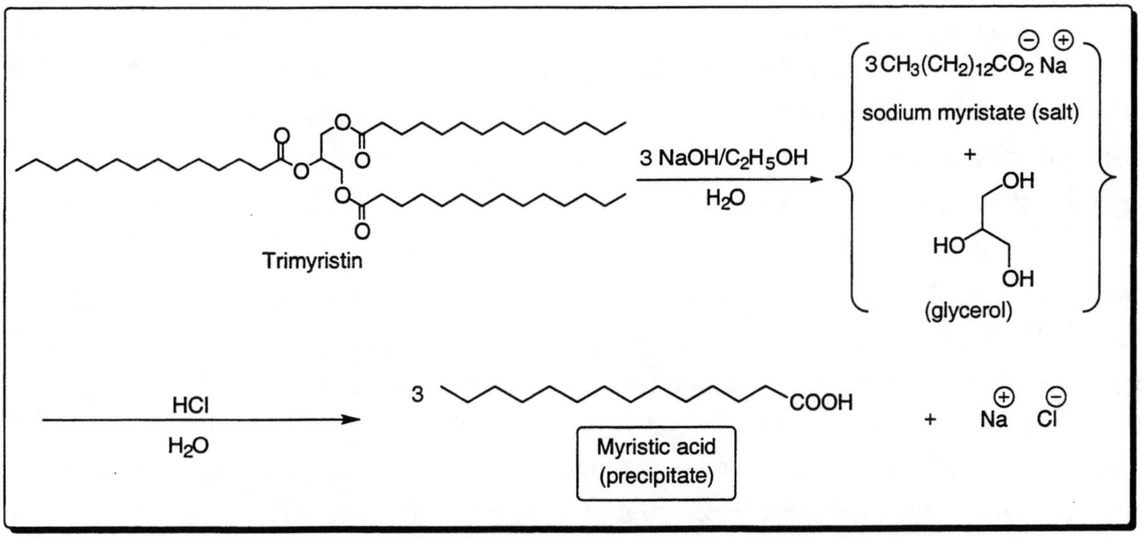

Scheme for the Synthesis of Myristic acid

Because there are literally millions of organic solids, some of them will of course have the same melting point. For example, trimyristin has the same melting point as myristic acid. How would one know that the product isolated at the end of this experiment is truly myristic acid and not unreacted trimyristin ? One can take a **mixed melting point** to answer this question. A mixed melting point depends on the fact that a pure sample melts at a high and sharp melting point temperature, and an impure one will melt at a lower and broad melting point. Thus, even though two different compounds happen to posses the same melting point, a mixture of the two of them in a 50:50 ratio, is regarded as an impure sample and it will behave accordingly.

III) Experimental Procedure

Assemble a micro-reflux apparatus as seen on the course web page. Use a sand bath on a hot plate as your heating source. Place in a 5 mL vial 100 mg of your recrystallized trimyristin from the previous lab. If you do not have a sufficient amount of trimyristin, obtain the difference from the stockroom. Add 1 mL of ethanol and 1 mL of 10% NaOH. Swirl to mix, and add a boiling stone. Connect the water hoses in the appropriate manner by allowing the water to flow in the bottom of the condenser and exit throughout the top. Allow a gentle stream to flow through the condenser. Too high a water pressure can force the hoses off, causing a flood. Reflux the mixture for one hour. The process of **refluxing** is commonly used in organic chemistry to speed a reaction to completion or to equilibrium by heating it at a constant temperature.

After one hour, turn off the heating source, remove the reaction from the hot plate and allow to cool to room temperature. Leave the condenser in place. In a 50 mL beaker, chill 5 mL of 10% HCl. Once the reaction is at ambient temperature, pour the solution into the cold acid and vigorously swirl as the precipitate forms. Check the pH of the solution using litmus paper. If the solution is not sufficiently acidic, add more HCl. Dilute the solution with 5 mL of cold water and collect the solid by vacuum filtration using a Hirsch funnel. Wet the filter disc first with two drops of water, and turn the water apirator on full force. Wash the acidic residues continuously with two 1 mL portions of cold water.

Save a few milligrams of the crude myristic acid for a melting point (spread the product on a watch glass to dry), and place the rest into a large test tube containing 3 ml of petroleum ether. Weigh a clean medium sized test tube. Prepare a filter pipet by using a boiling stick to push a small wad of cotton down into the top of the stem of the Pasteur pipet. Scoop up some Celite® into the pipet. Tap the bottom of the pipet carefully with your fingers. Obtain a height of about 1 inch. Using a second pipet, transfer a portion of the myristic acid solution into the filter pipet, the tip of which should be resting into the tared test tube.

Attach a rubber bulb to the top of the filter pipet and gently force the liquid through into the vial, by applying some pressure. Repeat until all the myristic acid solution has been filtered into the vial. Using a test tube holder, evaporate the solvent using a steam bath. Add a boiling stick. If an oil is observed, cool the product to room temperature and then place the product in an ice bath. Weigh the dry product. Determine the percent yield.

Take the melting point of the crude myristic acid and also the purified myristic acid. Compare and rationalize your results.

Take the melting point of your pure myristic acid, trimyristin and a well mixed 50:50 of the two. Record the data and interpret carefully.

IV) Post-Lab Report:

Include the following points in your Post-Lab Report:

• Base hydrolysis: Include the mechanism using the starting materials in this synthesis.

• A discussion of the concept of equilibrium as applied to this reaction (*e.g.* how to shift the equilibrium to make more product).

• A comparison of acid hydrolysis to base hydrolysis: conditions, etc…

• Alternative methods to base hydrolysis for the preparation of carboxylic acids.

• A discussion of mixed melting point: why it is used here and what information one can gain from it.

• Include any problems one might encounter in this experiment, and how one may suggest alternative methods to solve such problems.

Experiment 7: Synthesis and Reactivity of *tert*-Butyl Chloride *Via* an S$_N$1 Reaction

I) Aim of the Experiment

The purpose of this experiment is to synthesize *tert*-butyl chloride via an S$_N$1 reaction and to characterize it by simple chemical tests in order to describe its reactivity.

II) Introduction

Nucleophilic aliphatic substitution reactions constitute an important class of reactions in organic chemistry. The synthetic transformation of an alcohol into an alkyl halide is one representative process of this type. **Nucleophilic substitution** is a general reaction for aliphatic compounds in which the leaving group is attached to an sp^3-hybridized carbon; however, the mechanism for this given transformation depends inherently on the structure of the alkyl group bearing the leaving group. The two different mechanistic pathways that apply to substitution reactions are a **S$_N$1** or **S$_N$2** reaction. A S$_N$1 reaction is a nucleophilic substitution reaction, which is unimolecular. For these reactions, the rate-determining step (slow) involves only one molecule. A leaving group departs in the slow step to form a **carbocation** by ionization of the bond between the carbon and the leaving group. This step is assisted by employment of polar solvent. Since the relative stability of carbocations is tertiary > secondary > primary, the mechanism will take place most often on tertiary carbons. The nucleophile needs not be a strong one, since the difficult part of the reaction (formation of the carbocation) occurs before it attacks.

Tertiary alcohols can easily be converted to their corresponding alkyl chlorides by the addition of concentrated hydrochloric acid to the alcohol. Use of different reagents such as PCl_3 and $SOCl_2$ can be used in a similar fashion, however due to the highly toxic nature of these starting materials, and by-products, that are generated from the reaction, use of hydrochloric acid has become the common reagent of choice. In this experiment, concentrated hydrochloric acid is used to prepare *tert*-butyl chloride from *tert*-butyl alcohol.

The mechanism of this S_N1 reaction involves three steps. The first is a rapid (and reversible) protonation of the alcohol, followed by a much slower rate-determining step, the loss of water to give a relatively stable tertiary carbocation. In the final step, the carbocation is rapidly attacked by chloride ion to form the alkyl halide, which separates from the aqueous layer due to the fact that the product is insoluble in water.

There are several advantages to this experiment. First, it can be accomplished quickly without heating the reaction mixture. Secondly, no rearrangements of the incipient carbocation are seen to generate a mixture of products, which is a common phenomenon in carbocation chemistry.

III) Experimental Procedure

A) Synthesis of *tert*-Butyl chloride.

To a 60 mL separatory funnel, *carefully* add 15 mL of concentrated hydrochloric acid and 5 mL of *tert*-butyl alcohol. At this point, make sure the stopcock on the funnel does not leak. Swirl the contents of the funnel, place the stopper on, and invert it. Open the stopcock immediately to release excess pressure, pointing the funnel away from yourself and others. Shake the separatory funnel and vent it at regular intervals. Mount the funnel in a clamp or ring stand and allow the two layers to separate. Drain the lower aqueous layer into a 250 mL Erlenmeyer flask and discard it down the sink. Add 40 mL of saturated sodium bicarbonate solution to the crude *tert*-butyl chloride remaining in the separatory funnel. Gently swirl the funnel several times until bubbling ceases. Then, stopper the funnel, invert it, and open the stopcock immediately to release any pressure build up. Shake the funnel vigorously, opening the stopcock intermittently. Again, allow the layers to separate. Drain the aqueous (lower) layer into a 250 mL Erlenmeyer flask, and then wash the *tert*-butyl chloride remaining in the funnel with 30 mL of water. Again, drain the lower aqueous layer into a 250 mL Erlenmeyer flask and discard down the sink. Transfer the crude *tert*-butyl chloride to a 50 mL Erlenmeyer flask, add approximately 10 granules of anhydrous calcium chloride pellets to dry the product until the solution becomes clear. Decant or draw off the liquid using a pipet and transfer it to a 10 mL conical vial. Add a boiling stone and set up the apparatus for simple distillation. Distill and collect the steady boiling fraction between approximately 49-54 °C into a pre-weighed 10 mL collection vial. Place the collection vial in an ice bath throughout the distillation. As the distillation proceeds, if any lower boiling fraction is obtained, discard this fraction. After the distillation is complete, reweigh the product and calculate its percent yield. Proceed to part B for reactivity tests.

B) Qualitative Chemical Tests for Reactivity.

Since aliphatic halides are often initially detected by simple qualitative tests, it is not surprising that further characterization takes advantage that the halogen can be displaced. The two tests for displacing a halogen are complementary and useful in *classifying the structures of the alkyl halides*. The silver nitrate test proceeds via a carbocation process (e.g. S_N1) and the sodium iodide reaction by a direct displacement (S_N2).

1.) The Silver Nitrate (AgNO₃) Test.

When an alkyl halide is treated with a solution of $AgNO_3$ in ethanol, the silver ion initially coordinates with the halogen electron pair. This in turn weakens the carbon-halogen bond resulting in a molecule of insoluble silver halide, thus promoting an S_N1 reaction of the alkyl halide.

R—X: $\rightleftharpoons$ Ag $\overset{\oplus}{}$ $\longrightarrow$ R—X Ag $\longrightarrow$ R$\overset{\oplus}{}$ + AgX↓

Therefore, the order of reactivity for the AgNO$_3$ test is tertiary > secondary > primary. The solvent for the reaction is ethanol, which is polar, and it aids in the ionization of the halide. On the basis of this foregoing discussion, tertiary halides would be expected to react with silver nitrate most rapidly and primary halides least rapidly.

2.) Sodium Iodide (NaI) Test.

The sodium iodide test can be used to test for the presence of bromine or chlorine. Organic halides that can react by an S$_N$2 mechanism to give a precipitate of sodium halide salt (NaCl or NaBr) which is insoluble. The solvent for the reaction is acetone, which is a relatively nonpolar solvent and will dissolve NaI. Hence, the iodide anion is an excellent nucleophile in acetone, favoring the S$_N$2 reaction. Therefore, ionization of the halide does not occur. The order of reactivity for substrates is primary > secondary> tertiary. To elaborate further, primary alkyl chlorides or bromides react the most readily whereas tertiary substrates react the least.

NaI + R—Cl $\xrightarrow{\text{acetone}}$ R—I + NaCl↓

NaI + R—Br $\xrightarrow{\text{acetone}}$ R—I + NaBr↓

IV) Experimental Procedure for Chemical Tests.

Obtain a test tube rack and label 4 small test tubes. Into two test tubes add 0.1 mL of the synthesized *tert*-butyl chloride. Into the other two test tubes add 0.1 mL of 1-chlorobutane. To one test tube containing the *tert*-butyl chloride, add 1 mL of 18% solution of sodium iodide in acetone, stopper the test tube, and shake the contents vigorously. Note the time of first appearance of any precipitate. To the other test tube containing the synthesized product, add 1 mL of 1% ethanolic silver nitrate. Again, mix the contents well by shaking the test tube with a stopper. ***Avoid contact of AgNO₃ solution with the skin.*** Note the time of the addition of the silver nitrate as well as the first traces of any precipitate. If no reaction occurs within about 5 minutes standing at room temperature, heat the solution in the test tubes using a steam bath. *Exercise care not to over boil the solutions. Excessive heating causes loss of solvent.* If a precipitate forms, note its color and time it took to form.

To the test tubes containing the 1-chlorobutane, treat one test tube in the same manner above using the sodium iodide solution and the other with silver nitrate solution. Again, note times, and if precipitates form upon shaking. After 5 minutes if no solid forms heat the solution and note reactivity.

V) *Post-Lab Report.*

Discuss the following in your Post-Lab report.
• Nucleophilic substitution: Distinguish between S_N1 and S_N2. Address important aspects such as kinetics, solvent effects, leaving group ability, stereochemistry, order of reactivity for substrates, etc.
• Include a mechanism for the formation of *tert*-butyl chloride from the starting materials above.
• Explain the purpose of the qualitative chemical tests, and clearly analyze the results of the tests in correlation with what is expected. In addition, comment on the boiling point for further evidence of product identity and purity.
• Explain with regards to the reactivity tests of the following: Effect of structure on reactivity (that is, compare the tertiary halide *vs.* primary halide) in each of the test conditions. Point out the difference between both solvents used (solvent polarity), and comment on if any effect temperature had on the reaction.

Experiment 8: Bromination:
Synthesis of 1-Bromobutane from 1-Butanol

I) Aim of the Experiment

In this synthesis, you will use a mixture of sulfuric acid and sodium bromide to convert 1-butanol to 1-bromobutane via an S_N2 reaction, and analyze the product by refractive index.

$$\text{OH} \xrightarrow[\text{H}_2\text{SO}_4]{\text{NaBr}} \text{Br} + \text{H}_2\text{O} + \text{NaHSO}_4$$

bp 101-104 °C
$n_D = 1.4390$

II) Introduction

The conversion of alcohols to organic halides is an important step in a variety of syntheses. It is an extremely convenient and cheap transformation. Alkyl halides are probably the most important and generally useful intermediates used in organic reactions.

A variety of laboratory methods are available to perform the aforementioned transformation above. Three common reaction conditions for **bromination** of alcohols are as follows:

1) Heating the alcohol with aqueous hydrobromic acid (HBr), 2) A solution of HBr prepared by bubbling sulfur dioxide into bromine water, and 3) The method which we will use, is generating HBr *in situ* by use of an aqueous solution of sodium bromide, and excess sulfuric acid. This method is cheaper, and commonly preferred for safety reasons, and gives rise to the product in good yield.

The S_N1 reaction was introduced in the previous experiment, and as already stated because the hydroxide ion is such a poor leaving group, it is necessary to protonate the alcohol to produce a better leaving group, namely H_2O. Bromide ion is sufficiently nucleophilic and can displace the protonated hydroxyl group. You should think about the reaction mechanism carefully and draw a rationale mechanism for the reaction scheme.

37

You should also write a balanced chemical equation showing the reaction of NaBr and H_2SO_4 to generate HBr.

A variety of side reactions can occur when an alcohol becomes protonated. You should consider all possible side products that can be generated in this reaction, and note them accordingly in your report.

Besides postulating structures of side products and mechanisms of formation, you should also rationalize how one can obtain a good yield and purity of 1-bromobutane. Along with the experimental boiling point of 1-bromobutane, you will characterize the identity and purity of the product by **refractive index**. Refractive index is a physical property, like boiling point, and can be used in determining the identity and purity of a liquid. Refraction (bending of light) arises from the fact that light travels more slowly through a more dense substance. In organic chemistry, we are interested in the refraction of light as it passes through an organic liquid. The refractive index is measured with an instrument called a **refractometer**. Besides the wavelength of light used, refractive index values are temperature dependent. So, the temperature is always reported along with the value. Examples of the refractive index for benzene and ethanol are shown below.

benzene, n_D^{20} 1.5011

ethanol, n_D^{20} 1.3611

The refractive index is an extremely sensitive physical property. Unless the compound is extremely pure, it is almost impossible to duplicate the literature value exactly. However, the closer the observed value is to the reported value, the more pure the compound is likely to be. The refractive index, as stated above varies with temperature, so a correction factor must be applied to adjust the value to 20 °C. The equation is shown below.

$$n_D^{20} = n_D^{T} + 0.00045 \, (T\text{-}20 \, °C)$$
n= index of refraction
T=Temperature, °C

III) Experimental Procedure

Using a graduated pipet, measure out 1.5 mL of *n*-butanol and add it to a tared 10 mL conical vial. Re-weigh the vial to determine the exact weight. Add 2 g of sodium bromide and 2 mL of water. Cool the mixture in an ice bath and add 1.6 mL of concentrated sulfuric acid dropwise. *Be careful when handling concentrated sulfuric acid, it can cause severe burns.* Add a boiling stone and assemble a reflux apparatus. Use a water condenser and exert care on the proper method to connect the water hoses to the condenser. Be sure to place a moist cotton plug at the top of the water condenser. This moist cotton plug serves to trap any hydrogen bromide gas evolved during the reaction. Also, plug the cotton loosely, so that pressure does not build up in the reaction vessel.

Heat the mixture to a gentle boil for 30 minutes using a sand bath. After this time period, you should note two layers have formed. Allow the apparatus to cool to room temperature. Determine which layer will contain *n*-butyl bromide by adding a drop of water from a pipet. Which layer does the water droplet go to? Once you have determined which is the organic and which is the aqueous layer, remove the aqueous layer using a pipet, but do not remove any of the organic layer! If necessary, leave some of the aqueous layer behind. If solid material is present (salts), ignore it. If they are drawn up into the pipet, treat them as part of the aqueous layer.

Add 1 mL of H_2O to the reaction vial, which contains the organic layer. Cap the vial and shake gently. Occasionally vent the vial to release pressure build up. Any remaining salts should be dissolved in the water layer at this point. Allow the layers to separate. At this point, determine which layer is organic and which is aqueous.

Using a pipet, transfer the organic layer to a clean 10 mL conical vial. Add 1 mL of saturated sodium bicarbonate solution in increments, cap and shake vigorously for one minute. Allow to stand for several minutes so the mixture thoroughly separates. *Vent frequently to relieve any pressure that is produced.* Allow the layers to separate, then transfer the organic layer to a 5 mL conical vial using a pipet. At this point, the organic layer should be on the bottom. Add anhydrous sodium sulfate to dry the solution. Do not add too much drying agent. Consult your instructor for advice. Cap the vial and allow it to stand until the product appears clear and dry. When dry, transfer it to a clean 3 mL conical vial using a filter tip pipet and add a boiling stone. Distill the product using a clean dry Hickman still. Use aluminum foil for insulation. Record an approximate temperature each time the Hickman still becomes full, and transfer the distillate to a pre-weighed conical vial using a pipet. When distillation is complete (do not distill to dryness), weigh the vial and calculate the percent yield.

Analyze your distilled product by refractive index. Your instructor will show you how to operate the refractometer. Clean the prism section of the refractometer surface first with a lens-cleaning tissue and some solvent. Place one or two drops of 1-bromobutane on the prism and close the prism surface. Position the lamp to shine directly into the glass prism. Adjust the instrument by looking through the eyepiece and use the appropriate knobs to focus the cross hairs and to bring the light and dark areas into view. Move the dividing line between the dark and light areas exactly to the center of the cross hairs. Read the value and record the temperature. Compare this value to the literature value after the necessary correction factor has been applied. Comment in your post-lab report on the identity and purity of your synthesized product.

IV) *Post-Lab Report*

Discuss the following concepts in your Post-Lab report:
- Briefly distinguish between S_N1, S_N2, E1, and E2. Give examples and conditions.
- Show the mechanism for the formation of 1-bromobutane beginning from 1-butanol.
- Include in your report the optimum condtions for typical bromination of alcohols using these reagents.
- Balance the chemical equation for the reaction between sodium bromide and sulfuric acid.
- Discuss other bromination conditions for alcohols using different reagents.
- Include side reactions that can occur in this experiment.
- Clearly discuss if you obtained the product, 1-bromobutane, by interpreting the data and results above (use the bp and refractive index).

Experiment 9: Alkenes from Alcohols:
Analysis of a Mixture by Gas Chromatography

I) Aim of the Experiment

In this experiment, you will prepare a mixture of 2-methyl-butenes by acid catalyzed elimination of 2-methyl-2-butanol. The mixture of products will be separated and analyzed by gas chromatography.

2-methyl-2-butanol → 2-methyl-1-butene (bp 31 °C) + 2-methyl-2-butene (bp 39 °C)

II) Introduction

In the presence of strong acids, alcohols protonate to form a good leaving group, namely water. Upon loss of a proton adjacent to a good leaving group, an introduction of unsaturation (a double bond) can be performed. This is known as an **elimination reaction**. Specifically, proceeds through **E1 mechanism**.

Experimental evidence shows that this dehydration proceeds through a **carbocation** intermediate and the stability of the carbocation plays an important role in the amounts of alkenes formed.

In this experiment, you will dehydrate 2-methyl-2-butanol using a dilute sulfuric acid solution as a catalyst, giving rise to a mixture of alkenes. The two alkenes formed are a **trisubstituted alkene**, and a **disubstituted alkene**. You should thoroughly think through the mechanism (Push the ARROWS!), think about how each product forms and why the relative amounts of each are as such.

III) Experimental Procedure

Into a 10 mL conical vial, place 1.5 mL of distilled water, a boiling stone, and 1 mL of concentrated sulfuric acid. **CAUTION:** *Concentrated sulfuric acid causes severe burns, avoid contact with your skin and clothes.* Swirl to mix the reactants and cool the solution in an ice bath. To the cold solution, with swirling, add 2 mL of 2-methyl-2-butanol. Set up the apparatus for simple distillation as shown on the course web page. Do not use the fractional distillation set-up. Into another 10 mL collection vial, place a few pellets (~10) of calcium chloride, and weigh the vial with the screw cap. Remove the screw cap, attach the receiver to the distillation apparatus, and cool the receiver in ice to avoid loss of the very volatile products. Heat the vial using a sand bath and a hot plate. Turn the heat setting up until very small bubbles begin to appear in the reaction vial, then turn down the heat so that the solution refluxes slowly. *It is very important to control the heat*, so during the distillation only tiny bubbles appear in the reaction vial. If the bubbling becomes too vigorous and the bubbles are too large, both water and alcohol will begin to distill over. Distill the mixture and collect the products over the temperature range of 30-40 °C. Keep the distillate temperature below 40 °C. When all the products have distilled, you will notice a drop in temperature, and the walls of the Claisen adapter will become cloudy. Stop the distillation. Remove the collection vial, place the screw cap on the vial to prevent the evaporation of the product and re-weigh the product. Calculate the percent yield of the butenes (together). Analyze the product by gas chromatography.

IV) Gas Chromatography (GC)

Gas chromatography, as in other forms of chromatography, is a good method for determining purity and analyzing mixtures. The instrument used is known as a **chromatograph** and the printout is called a **chromatogram**.

As in TLC, each spot indicates an individual compound present. In GC, each peak that appears at a characteristic position indicates a particular compound. GC is a good way to determine the identity of a compound if a known sample is available for comparison.

In GC, the stationary phase is usually a non-volatile liquid (high boiling point). This liquid is coated usually on a solid support and packed into a tube to form a column. A flow of inert gas, usually helium, serves as the mobile phase. Using a syringe, the mixture is injected into the chromatograph. The compound is vaporized and passes into the column where separation occurs. The components of the mixture separate themselves based on polarity, temperature, and rate of gas flow through the column. A sample chromatogram is shown below. Your instructor will provide a further discussion on theory and GC interpretation.

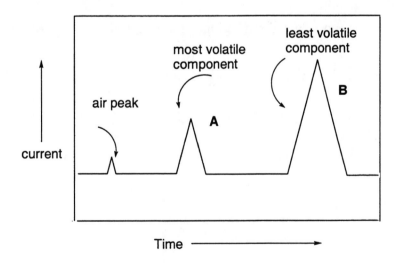

Gas chromatogram

V) Experimental Procedure for GC

With the aid of your instructor, you are now ready to analyze and separate the mixture using a GC. Obtain a clean syringe from the stockroom. *Be careful when handling these syringes, they are fragile and expensive.* Inject 1 μL of the mixture into the gas chromatograph (Gow MAC model 650). This model contains a nonpolar column and an oven set to room temperature. Write down the G.C. conditions in your notebook (column temperature, detector temperature, etc.) Run the chromatogram, and calculate the percentage of each component present in the mixture. Interpret the chromatogram and rationalize which peaks are which, and the relative concentration of each.

VI) Post-Lab Report

Discuss the following in your Post-Lab report:
- Elimination reactions: Distinguish between E1 and E2. Give examples and discuss reaction conditions, stability of carbocations, etc.
- Explain Zaitsev's rule and relate this concept to the experiment.
- Discuss briefly gas chromatography: theory, purpose, conditions, etc.
- Report the yield of the butenes together, and analyze the gas chromatogram.
- Clearly rationalize the product distribution. Include a discussion of thermodynamic stability.
- Show the mechanism for this reaction and possible side products that can result using these conditions.

I) Aim of the Experiment

The purpose of this experiment is to prepare cyclohexene from cyclohexanol and characterize the product by simple chemical tests.

II) Introduction

We have seen in the previous experiment that when an alcohol is heated in the presence of a strong acid, the major product formed is an alkene or a mixture of alkenes. The acid is essential because it converts the very poor leaving group (-OH) into a reasonably good one, namely water. Loss of a proton from the intermediate (**elimination**) brings about the formation of an alkene.

Before the invention of modern instrumentation such as spectroscopy, organic chemists relied heavily on **qualitative chemical tests** to determine if functional groups were present in molecules, or if a chemical reaction had occurred. Two simple chemical tests can quickly distinguish alkenes from other functional groups. Almost all alkenes react quickly and smoothly with a dilute solution of bromine (red) to form a colorless solution. Similarly, alkenes react with a solution of potassium permanganate (purple) to discharge its color and produce a muddy brown precipitate (MnO_2). These two reactions are an example of an **addition reaction.** An addition reaction results in the conversion of one π bond and one σ bond into two σ bonds. The electrons of the π bond are exposed and are particularly susceptible to electron-seeking reagents (electrophiles), such as bromine and potassium permangante.

(Colorless)   ← Br_2 (Red) ← [cyclohexene] → $KMnO_4$ (Purple) → [cyclohexanediol] OH OH (Colorless) + MnO_2 (Brown) ↓

III) Experimental Procedure

Into a tared 10 mL conical vial, place 2 mL of cyclohexanol. Reweigh the vial to determine the exact mass of the alcohol. Add 0.5 mL of 85 % phosphoric acid and eight drops of concentrated sulfuric acid to the vial. You should begin to see a yellowish color developing. Swirl the vial to mix the viscous liquids and add a boiling stone. Attach a Hickman still to the vial and leave the top of the still open to the atmosphere. Place your thermometer into the center of the Hickman still. Lower the vial into the sand bath and heat the mixture until the product begins to distill. Heat the mixture at such a slow rate that the distillation requires about 45 minutes. Be aware that this is not a "normal" distillation in which we are purifying a liquid. In this case we are distilling cyclohexene as it is being formed, so the process will be slower than a normal distillation. As the cyclohexene distills, record the boiling range in your notebook. However, be aware cyclohexene may not distill at its normal boiling point. Several factors such as quick heating and an inaccurate thermometer position may effect this reading. Remove the distillate from the well of the Hickman still head using a Pasteur pipet when necessary, entering the apparatus through the side arm of the still. Transfer the distillate to a 5 mL conical vial and cap. Continue the distillation until no more liquid will distill. *DO NOT DISTILL TO DRYNESS!*

When the distillation is complete, remove the remaining distillate from the reservoir of the Hickman still and transfer it to the 5 mL vial containing the previous distillate. Using a pipet, add 2 mL of saturated sodium chloride solution to the Hickman still head in portions, taking care to rinse the inside walls. This addition of salt water is a technique known as **"salting-out"**. Salting-out decreases the solubility of an organic compound in water. Do this carefully, washing any remaining product down into the well. Transfer this liquid to the capped 5 mL vial containing the distilled product.

Shake the mixture in the capped vial. Remove and discard the bottom aqueous layer using a pipet. Add a small spatula full of anhydrous Na_2SO_4 to the organic layer. Place the cap on the vial and set it aside for 15 minutes.

46

Transfer as much dried liquid as possible, leaving the solid behind to a clean pre-weighed 3 mL vial and weigh with a screw cap. Weigh the product and calculate the percentage yield.

IV) Chemical Tests for Unsaturation

Into two small test tubes, place ~4 drops of cyclohexanol in each. Into another pair of small test tubes, place ~4 drops of cyclohexene that you synthesized. Clearly label the test tubes. To one test tube from each group (alcohol + alkene), add dropwise bromine in dichloromethane. *Be careful when handling bromine solution, it can cause severe burns. Also do not breathe its vapors.* While swirling, continually add drop by drop until the red color is no longer present. Record the result in each case.

To the two remaining test tubes, perform the same procedure as above, however, use the solution of potassium permanganate. Record and rationalize your results.

V) Post-Lab Report:

Include the following key points in the theoretical background of your Post-Lab report:
• Differences between elimination and addition reactions. Illustrate using pertinent examples.
• Mechanism of the elimination reaction of cyclohexanol to produce cyclohexene in the presence of sulfuric acid.
• The mechanisms for both the addition of bromine and potassium permanganate to cyclohexene.
• Include other examples of addition reactions in organic chemistry.
• Purpose of catalytic vs. stoichiometric amount of a reagent.
• Discuss the purpose of the qualitative analysis tests performed in this experiment. Analyze the results and compare them to the literature.
• Include possible experimental errors and suggest alternatives to solving such problems.
• In the discussion section of your report, clearly convey the product namely cyclohexene, was indeed synthesized using the data above.

Experiment 11: Spectroscopy-Infrared Spectroscopy and Nuclear Magnetic Resonance Spectroscopy

I) Aim of the Experiment

The purpose of this experiment is to obtain and interpret infrared spectra of variety of liquid organic samples and of an unknown compound.

II) Introduction

After a compound has been synthesized, isolated, and purified, its identity must be verified. This is best accomplished by comparing its physical properties (melting points, boiling points, refractive index and so on) with the literature values. Qualitative chemical tests also provide important information as well, such as the presence of certain functional groups (for example, decolorization with Br_2 indicates the presence of double bonds). These qualitative tests usually require very large amounts of the compound, and often expose you to toxic reagents. Therefore, this will not be a focus of this course. However, **spectroscopy,** is of great help to verify the identity of a compound prepared in the laboratory. Various spectroscopic procedures are available to an organic chemist that unambiguously and confidently identify the presence of functional groups, and allows the chemist to postulate the compounds complete structure. We will focus on 2 spectroscopic techniques in this course: *Infrared* (IR) *Spectroscopy* and *Nuclear Magnetic Resonance* (^{1}H NMR) *Spectroscopy* .

III) Infrared Spectroscopy

The presence and also the environment of functional groups in organic molecules can be identified by infrared spectroscopy. Infrared radiation, which is electromagnetic radiation of longer wavelengths than visible light, is detected not by the eyes, but by the feeling of warmth on the skin. When absorbed by molecules, radiation of this wavelength (~2.5-15 microns), increase the amplitude of vibrations of the chemical bond joining atoms together.

Infrared spectra are measured in units called **frequency** or **wavelength**. The wavelength is measured in micrometers (μm). The positions of the absorption band, often are very characteristic of individual functional groups, which is measured in frequency units known as wavenumbers (γ) which is the reciprocal of centimeters (cm^{-1}).

Every compound has its own unique characteristic IR spectrum, like a fingerprint. The region where IR light is transmitted through a sample is called the **"baseline"**. Regions where IR light is absorbed by the sample are called **"peaks"** or **"bands"**.

When the frequency of the infrared light is the same as the natural vibrational frequency of the atomic bond, light will be absorbed by the molecule and the amplitude of the bond vibration will increase. These vibrations are generally expressed as the bond **stretching** or **bending**. The regions where these stretches occur in the spectrum can lead to the successful assignment of principal functional groups in a molecule and ultimately to its structure.

IV) Analysis of Infrared Spectra

Three rules apply to all IR analyses:
I) Pay close attention to the strongest absorptions, "peaks".
II) Pay most attention to peaks to the left of 1250 cm^{-1} in the spectra.
III) Pay attention to the absence of certain peaks and to the presence of others.

Tables of IR characteristic frequencies can be very lengthy. We will provide a short concise table of fundamental infrared absorption frequencies as well as a "road map" you may use to interpret spectra.

A good way to start the analysis of an infrared spectrum is with the carbonyl stretching region. To guide you through the analysis, we have prepared a flow chart. This scheme is not infallible, but will be far superior to random guessing. Although conclusions of the scheme used are stated firmly, confirmation of your spectrum to the literature match is desirable. With the aid of your instructor you will interpret several examples of infrared spectra.

V) Experimental Procedure

The instructor will show the students how to run the IR spectrophotometer. The student should be aware for the future of the individual steps in obtaining a spectrum. Most cases in this course, you will take IR spectra of liquids. Solids and gases can be done, but we will save these for more advanced classes. With pure liquid samples, the simplest technique is to prepare a thin film between a pair of NaCl salt plates. This method of examination is regarded to as "neat". One may obtain a spectrum of a compound in solution, but for ease of simplicity in procedure, we will use the common thin film procedure.

Using a Pasteur pipet (clean and dry), place a drop of your sample in the center of one plate. Place the second plate gently on top, *be careful, they are expensive and fragile*. Hold the salt plates by the edges and avoid getting oils from your skin on the plates. The sandwich is then pressed together to produce an even film of liquid. Obtain the infrared spectrum as noted by the instructor. Clean the salt plates with dichloromethane or a good grade of acetone. **CAUTION: Do not use water to clean the salt plates !** Wipe the plates clean using Kimwipes and return them to the stockroom. Begin interpreting your spectrum using the tables provided.

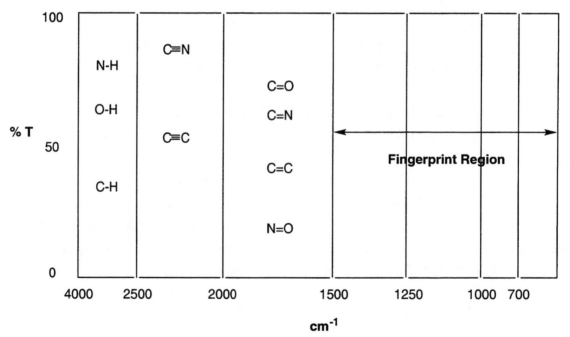

Regions of characteristic infrared absorptions of common functional groups

Characteristic Infrared Absorption Frequencies

Peak Position (cm^{-1})	Functional Group	Features
3600-3200	Alcohol O-H N-H	Often broad NH$_2$ often 2 peaks N-H one
3400-2500	Carboxylic Acid O-H	Strong, very broad, often more than one peak
3050-3000	Aromatic C-H Alkenyl C-H	
3000-2800	Alkyl C-H	
2900, 2700	Aldehyde C-H	Sharp, 2 bands often weak
2260-2215	C≡N	Strong and very sharp
2150-2100	C≡C	If terminal-strong, sharp if internal-weak
1720-1710	C=O	Strong, sharp. Position dependent on type of C=O function and degree of unsaturation. Conjugation can lower by 20-60 cm^{-1}
1650	Alkenyl C=C	Lowered by conjugation, may be weak
1600-1450	Aromatic C=C	Usually 2-3 sharp peaks
1520-1350	NO$_2$	2 Intense bands
1200-1050	—C-O—	C-O Stretching single bond characteristic to esters, ethers and alcohols

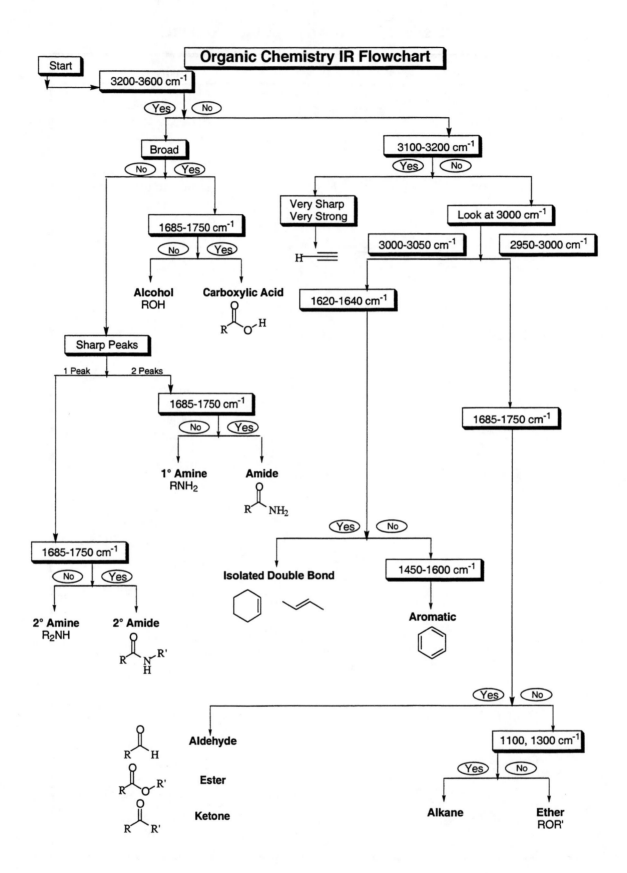

Organic Chemistry IR Flowchart

Start

3200-3600 cm⁻¹ — Yes / No

Broad — No / Yes

3100-3200 cm⁻¹ — Yes / No

Very Sharp Very Strong

Look at 3000 cm⁻¹

1685-1750 cm⁻¹ — No / Yes

3000-3050 cm⁻¹

2950-3000 cm⁻¹

Alcohol
ROH

Carboxylic Acid

1620-1640 cm⁻¹

Sharp Peaks — 1 Peak / 2 Peaks

1685-1750 cm⁻¹ — No / Yes

1685-1750 cm⁻¹

1° Amine
RNH₂

Amide

Yes / No

1685-1750 cm⁻¹ — No / Yes

1450-1600 cm⁻¹

Isolated Double Bond

2° Amine
R₂NH

2° Amide

Aromatic

Yes / No

Aldehyde

1100, 1300 cm⁻¹ — Yes / No

Ester

Ketone

Alkane

Ether
ROR'

52

Spectroscopy: Nuclear Magnetic Resonance Spectroscopy (NMR)

I) *Aim of the Experiment*

In this experiment, you will determine the chemical structure of several organic molecules by interpreting their proton nuclear magnetic resonance spectrum (^{1}H NMR).

II) *Introduction*

Previously, above we discussed infrared spectroscopy. This section describes the complimentary technique of **nuclear magnetic resonance** or **NMR**, which is useful for identifying molecules chemical structure. Many types of NMR are known, but we will only be concerned with proton NMR in this part of the course.

Proton nuclear magnetic resonance spectroscopy (^{1}H NMR) provides a powerful tool for determining the *number*, *kind*, and *relative locations* of *hydrogen atoms* in a molecule. Three basic kinds of information can be used in characterizing or identifying an unknown compound. Further detail will be provided in the organic lecture course.

A) The signal strength, or **peak area**, as measured by the **integral** (the stair-step line over the peaks) is directly proportional to the number of identical protons in the sample that produced the signal. Different protons give different peaks.

B) The position of the peak in the spectrum, or the **chemical shift**, is determined by the atom or structural grouping, to which the proton is bonded. Chemical shifts of protons in the sample will be measured relative to an internal standard (**Tetramethylsilane or TMS**) at 0.00 ppm.

C) Because of coupling (proton-proton interactions), a signal may be split into several peaks. The number (**multiplicity**) and separation of these peaks imply characteristics of certain protons and structures. In general, molecules containing a given set of protons will appear as (n+1) peaks if they are adjacent to (n) protons. The distance between adjacent peaks are known as the **coupling constant** (*J*).

53

III) Interpretation

Learning to analyze ^{1}H NMR spectra requires studying a number of known examples and then practicing with some unknowns. Listed below are some helpful tips to make your spectral interpretation easier. You will review several examples with the aid of your instructor.

A.) Using the integration for each peak or multiplet, to determine the number of protons represented by each peak or multiplet. The relative number of protons must always be a whole number. If the molecular formula is given, the relative number of protons should equal the total number of protons in the formula.

B.) If the molecular formula is given to you, determine the **units of unsaturation** as compared to the open chain saturated molecule (C_nH_{2n+2}). Any difference suggests the possibility of double, triple or aromatic double bonds.

C.) You should learn to recognize methyl, ethyl, isopropyl, *tert*-butyl, and other characteristic groups. Thus, a singlet of three protons is a methyl group. A quartet of two protons and a triplet of three protons would be an ethyl group, a singlet of nine protons would be a *tert*-butyl group. The splitting pattern follows the n+1 rule.

D.) Subtract the known portions of the molecule from the molecular formula, if given. This will allow you to assign the remaining protons.

E.) Absorptions around δ 7 to 8 ppm suggest an aromatic ring present in the molecule.

F.) Absorptions seen δ 5 to 6 ppm suggest vinyl protons. The coupling contant will help you determine the stereochemistry of the double bond, namely *cis* or *trans*.

G.) A broad singlet of one proton at a chemical shift of δ 10 ppm or more suggests the presence of a carboxylic acid.

H.) A broadened singlet between δ 1-5 ppm might be due to the OH group of an alcohol or the NH group of an anime.

I.) Absorptions around δ 9-10 ppm integrating to one proton suggest an aldehyde. However, this peak is **not** broadened as in the carboxylic acid case.

J.) A singlet at δ 2.5 suggests an aliphatic alkyne. Aromatic alkynes absorb slightly further down field.

K.) Absorptions around δ 2-2.3 suggest protons on the carbon atom adjacent to a carbonyl group (*i.e.*, methyl ketone).

L.) Absorption around δ 2.8-4.5 ppm suggests a proton on a carbon bearing a highly electronegative element such as oxygen, nitrogen, or a halogen. The molecular formula will confirm the presence if an atom is present.

M.) Use the chemical shift values seen in the table below to confirm the presence of specific functional groups.

Typical Chemical Shifts for Types of Hydrogen Atoms in the ^{1}H NMR

Type of Hydrogen Atom	δ^*	Type of Hydrogen Atom	δ^*
$(CH_3)_4Si$	0.0	$ROCH_3$, R–C–OCH$_3$ (O)	3.8
RCH_3	0.9	$R_2C{=}CH_2$	5.0
RCH_2R (acyclic)	1.3	H, R / C=C / R, R	5.3
(cyclic)	1.5	Ar–H	7.3
R_3CH	1.5-2.0	R–C(O)–H	9.7
R, CH$_3$ / C=C / R, R'	1.8	R–NH$_2$ (variable)	1-3
R–C(O)–CH$_3$	2.0-2.3	Ar–NH$_2$	3-5
Ar–CH$_3$	2.3	R–C(O)–N(H)–R	5-9
R≡H	2.5	R–OH (variable)	1-5
$RNHCH_3$	2-3	Ar–OH	4-7
RCH_2X	3.5	R–C(O)–OH	10-13

* The chemical shift values are given in ppm relative to an internal standard, TMS, at 0.00 ppm and are for hydrogen atoms shown in bold. These values might shift slightly with changes in solvent, temperature and concentration.

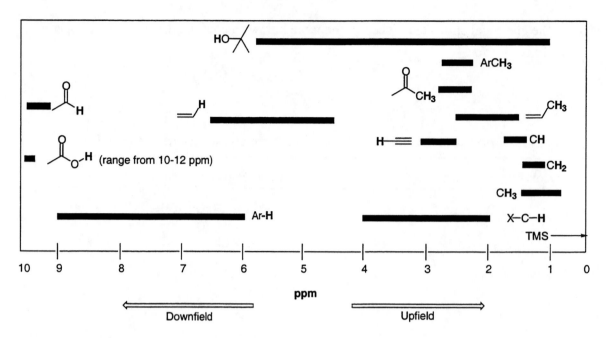

Characteristic ranges of various types of protons in ^{1}H NMR spectra.

IV) Post-Lab Report

No Post-Lab reports are due for this experiment. However, your instructor will hand you out a problem set containing several IR and ^{1}H NMR spectra. This problem set will ask you to solve and deduce the structure of several organic molecules based on interpretation of the spectra. Complete the assignment as indicated in the directions, and turn them in on the next lab meeting.

Chapter 3

Organic Chemistry Laboratory II
Experiments

Organic Chemistry Laboratory II Syllabus

In organic lab 2, you will apply the techniques learned in organic lab 1, to new problems. This course will focus on a synthetic perspective using fundamental named organic reactions applied to the transformation of one material into another. Students are advised to understand, prior to coming to the lab, what they will perform in practice, and they are also strongly encouraged to use a problem solving approach during the class as well as while writing post lab reports. Scientific organization and writing will be other goals of this course.

Schedule of Experiments

Lab Meeting # 1   Check-in and Safety lecture.

Lab Meeting # 2   Exp. 1: Diels-Alder Reaction-Preparation of 9,10-Dihydroanthracene-9,10-α,β-Succinic Acid Anhydride.

Lab Meeting # 3   Exp. 2: Oxidation of Borneol.

Lab Meeting # 4   Exp. 3: Stereoselective Reduction of Camphor.

Lab Meeting # 5   Exp. 4: Esterification: Synthesis of Methyl Benzoate.

Lab Meeting # 6   Exp. 5: Nitration of Methyl Benzoate.

Lab Meeting # 7	Exp. 6: Friedel-Crafts Acylation of Ferrocene.
Lab Meeting # 8	Exp. 7: Preparation of a 2,4-Dinitrophenylhydrazone Derivative of an Unknown Aldehyde or Ketone.
Lab Meeting # 9	Exp. 8: Grignard Synthesis of Triphenylmethanol.
Lab Meeting # 10	Exp. 9: Wittig Reaction-Synthesis of trans-9-(2-phenylethenyl) anthracene.
Lab Meeting # 11	Exp. 10: Synthesis of Dibenzalacetone by the Aldol Condensation.
Lab Meeting # 12	Exp. 11: Enzymatic Reactions-Enzymatic Reduction of a Ketone to a Chiral Alcohol.
Lab Meeting *# 13*	***Make-up Lab.***
Lab Meeting # 14	Check-out and Clean up.

Experiment 1: Diels-Alder Reaction: Preparation of 9,10-Dihydroanthracene-9,10-α,β-Succinic Acid Anhydride

I) Aim of the Experiment

The purpose of this experiment is to synthesize 9,10-Dihydroanthracane-9,10-α,β-Succinic Acid Anhydride via a Diels-Alder reaction.

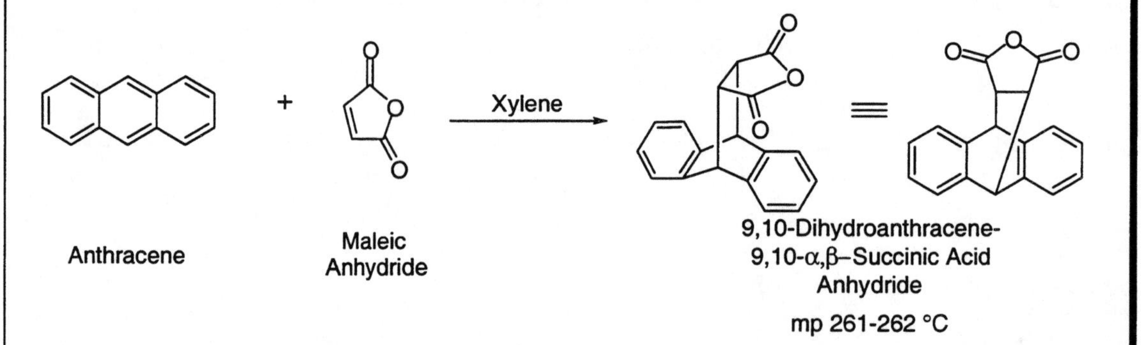

Anthracene + Maleic Anhydride → (Xylene) → 9,10-Dihydroanthracene-9,10-α,β–Succinic Acid Anhydride

mp 261-262 °C

II) Introduction

The Diels-Alder reaction is one of the most powerful synthetic conversions in organic chemistry. It is an example of a [4+2] cycloaddition reaction between a **diene** and a **dienophile,** which leads to the formation of 6-membered cyclic rings, as illustrated below. The Diels-Alder reaction can proceed thermally (heat) or photochemically (light), by way of a **concerted**, single-step mechanism. With cycloaddition reactions, it is common to be concerned with the overlap between the atomic orbitals of the **HOMO** (Highest Occupied Molecular Orbital) of the diene and with the **LUMO** (Lowest Unoccupied Molecular Orbital) of the dienophile.

The facile reaction proceeds best if the dienophile contains **electron-withdrawing groups (EWG)**, such as a carbonyl groups or a cyano group attached to the π bond and if the diene contains **electron-donating groups (EDG),** such as alkyl.

When a cyclic diene and a cyclic dienophile react with each other, more than one stereoisomer may be formed. The reaction is highly stereospecific and the isomer that predominates is the one that involves the maximum overlap of π electrons in the transition state. The transition state for the formation of the *endo* stereochemistry is favored in the product over the *exo* stereochemistry. Consider the reaction below between cyclopentadiene and maleic anhydride.

The *endo* isomer is present as the predominat product since the overlap of the π electrons is greatest. In the *exo* product, the overlap is not as great.

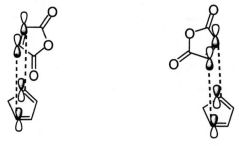

endo transition state   *exo* transition state

In the following reaction, you will synthesize 9,10-dihydroanthracane-9,10-α,β-succinic acid anhydride. Maleic anhydride serves as the dienophile in this case and the double bonds in the central ring of anthracene functionality serve as the diene. The central ring of anthracene has a characteristic diene system and thus reacts to form stable adducts with dieneophiles at the 9 and 10 positions. You should consider why these double bonds are the most reactive.

III) Experimental Procedure

Into a 3 mL conical vial, place a boiling stone, 80 mg of anthracene and 40 mg of maleic anhydride. In the hood, add 1.0 mL of dry xylene. Attach an air condenser and place the apparatus in a sand bath and heat to vigorous reflux for about 30 minutes. During this time, you should see the yellow color of the mixture disappear. Allow the mixture to cool to room temperature and then place the vial in an ice bath for approximately 10 minutes, at which point the product should form crystals.

Collect the product by vacuum filtration using a Hirsch funnel and wash the product with 0.5 mL of cold xylene. Place the product on a watch glass with some paraffin film shavings to absorb the xylene. Keep the crystals and the paraffin separate. Cover with another watch glass.

Dry the crystals over one week time period in your drawer. Xylene is a high boiling hydrocarbon solvent and it is difficult to remove. Xylene is readily absorbed by paraffin, hence the reason for placing it on the watch glass with the crystals. The next lab period, weigh the product, calculate the percent yield and the melting point. Compare the melting point to the literature value. Hand in your lab report one week later.

IV) *Post-Lab Report*

In your Post-Lab write-up, include the following key points in your theoretical background section.

- A discussion of the Diels-Alder reaction: theory, conditions, its synthetic utility, general requirements and rules, etc.
- A clear explanation of the stereochemistry control in the Diels-Alder reaction. Discuss *endo-exo* isomers, electronic factors such as electron-donating and electron-withdrawing substituents on the diene and the dienophile, orbital interaction, etc.
- Show the mechanism of the reaction.
- Discuss important side reactions that can occur in this experiment.
- Discuss if the product was formed in the reaction, and how you determined this.

Experiment 2: Oxidation of Borneol

I) Aim of the Experiment

In this experiment, you will perform an oxidation reaction involving the interconversion of borneol to camphor using sodium hypochlorite (bleach).

Borneol $\xrightarrow[\text{CH}_3\text{CO}_2\text{H}]{\text{NaOCl}}$ Camphor

II) Introduction

Alcohols that have a hydrogen adjacent to a hydroxyl (OH) group (an α-hydrogen) can be easily oxidized to a carbonyl compound.

Secondary alcohol $\xrightarrow{\text{oxidation}}$ ketone

If the alcohol is primary, then upon oxidation, an aldehyde results, which can be further oxidized to the carboxylic acid. Oxidation of a secondary alcohol will give rise to a ketone, and further oxidation presents no problem.

A wide variety of oxidizing agents are known and are readily available to an organic chemist. Some of these oxidizing agents contain transition metals which are often expensive and toxic, presenting disposal problems. An excellent alternative is use of commercially available sodium hypochlorite (bleach) since this reagent possesses lower toxicity and is more environmentally friendly.

When sodium hypochlorite is added to acetic acid, an acid-base reaction takes place, giving rise to hypochlorous acid (HOCl), which serves as a source of positive chlorine ions (Cl^+) known as the **chloronium ion**. This oxidizing agent is a strong electrophile and the ion is readily transferred to the substrate to be oxidized.

$$NaOCl + CH_3CO_2H \longrightarrow HOCl + CH_3CO_2^{\ominus} \, Na^{\oplus}$$

The mechanism of the reaction is not fully understood, however, chemists are sure that it does not proceed via a free radical reaction. It may form an intermediate alkyl hypochlorite ester (R-O-Cl), which by an E2 elimination gives rise to the ketone and releases the chloride ion. However, you should suggest a reasonable mechanism in your report for the formation of the product. Consult a variety of references to help you in this.

To ensure that complete oxidation occurs, it is necessary to have an excess of sodium hypochlorite in the reaction. Since concentrations of this reagent may vary in the brand of bleach used, you must use a simple test (starch-iodide) to see if hypochlorite is present by noting a color change using an indicator paper.

$$OCl^{\ominus} + 2I^{\ominus} + 2H^{\oplus} \longrightarrow Cl^{\ominus} + I_2 + H_2O$$

III) Experimental Procedure

To a 5 mL conical vial, add 0.18 g of borneol, 0.5 mL of acetone, .15 mL of glacial acetic acid and a spin vane. The borneol is racemic in which it possesses both *cis* and *trans* isomers of the alcohol. Even though the reaction begins as a mixture of starting materials, upon oxidation, only one product is obtained, namely the ketone.

Attach an air condenser to the vial and clamp the apparatus to a ring stand in a warm water bath of about 50 °C. Heat the water using a hot plate equipped with stirring. Do not warm the water bath above this temperature during the reaction. An ideal reaction temperature is between 45-50 °C (use a thermometer). While in the water bath, stir the reaction until the borneol dissolves.

While stirring the reaction mixture, add dropwise 2 mL of bleach solution (5.25 % sodium hypochlorite) through the top of the air condenser over a thirty-minute time period. *Be careful not to get this reagent on your clothes.* When the addition is complete, stop the stirring and using a pipet, remove a few drops of the aqueous layer and place these droplets onto a moist piece of starch-iodine paper. If there is no color change, add another 0.2 mL of the bleach solution to the vial and stir several more minutes. Repeat the test again. Continue this procedure until you receive a positive starch-iodine test, as indicated by the paper turning blue-black in color. Stir the mixture for an additional ten minutes after the last addition of the bleach and repeat the test again. It should still be positive (blue-black color) or repeat as stated above. Stir the mixture for ten minutes.

When the reaction is complete, allow to cool to room temperature by removing the vial from the water bath, and remove the air condenser. Add 1 mL of dichloromethane to the vial, cap, and shake with occasional venting. Remove the spin vane using forceps and rinse with a few drops of dichloromethane. Using a pipet, remove the lower organic layer and transfer it into another 5 mL conical vial. Extract the aqueous layer with another 1 mL portion of dichloromethane and combine it with the first organic layer.

Wash the organic layer with 1 mL of saturated sodium bicarbonate solution. Use a Pasteur pipet to draw the liquid up and down in the vial a few times. After the majority of the bubbling ceases, cap the vial, shake, and vent frequently to release the pressure. Allow to stand for ten minutes. *Carefully*, remove the aqueous layer (top), and discard. Wash the organic solution with 1 mL of saturated sodium bisulfite solution and 1 mL of water. What is the purpose of each of these washings? Using a pipet, transfer the organic layer to a test tube and dry for ten minutes using anhydrous sodium sulfate. Shake the test tube occasionally.

To a tared 10 or 25 mL Erlenmeyer flask, transfer the dried organic layer using a filter pipet and rinse the drying agent twice with 1 mL portions of dichloromethane. Combine all the layers into the flask and add a boiling stone and evaporate the solvent in a hood using a hot plate set low (~50 °C).

When the solvent has been removed, you should see a solid residue. Remove the flask from the heat immediately or your product may be lost due to sublimation. Re-weigh the cool flask and determine the percent yield of your camphor. Note the odor.

Obtain an IR spectrum of your product (thin-film), interpret the spectrum carefully, and compare it to the literature spectrum. Store the camphor in a clean tightly sealed vial until the next lab period.

IV) Post-Lab Report

In your Post-Lab report discuss the following points.

- Oxidations in organic chemistry, general trends, and different oxidizing agents that can be used for this transformation other than using sodium hypochlorite.
- Include the mechanism of the reaction to produce camphor starting from borneol.
- Side reactions that can occur in this experiment.
- Clearly convey that the oxidation in the above reaction did in fact occur in your discussion section based on the results. Interpret the infrared spectrum carefully, and compare it to the starting material spectrum (use literature). Discuss the presence and absence of functional groups appropriately. Compare the IR spectrum of the experimental product to the literature spectrum. Attach a copy of the spectrum to your post-lab report. A common source available to find literature IR spectra is using the Sadtler or Aldrich library of Infrared spectra available in the Library.

Experiment 3: Stereoselective Reduction of Camphor

I) Aim of the Experiment

The purpose of this experiment is to reduce the camphor synthesized in Experiment 2, using sodium borohydride to give an isomeric alcohol isoborneol. The relative percentages of the isoborneol and borneol will be obtained via ^1H NMR.

Camphor — NaBH$_4$ / CH$_3$OH → Isoborneol

II) Introduction

Nucleophilic addition of the hydride ion (H$^-$) to the carbonyl group results in the reduction of aldehydes to primary alcohols, and as in this experiment, ketones to secondary alcohols. Common reducing agents used in the organic lab are sodium borohydride (NaBH$_4$) and lithium aluminum hydride (LiAlH$_4$). Both reagents have a (H$^-$) ion as the anion, which is a powerful base as well as a nucleophile. In this experiment, we will use sodium borohydride since it is easier to handle than its counterpart LiAlH$_4$ which reacts more violently with water.

You should propose an acceptable mechanism in your report for the action of sodium borohydride in reducing the ketone camphor to the corresponding alcohol.

The stereochemistry of the reduction is a very interesting problem and the exact reason for stereochemical control in reduction reactions is quite controversial among organic chemists. Some organic chemists believe an **electronic factor** dictates the stereochemical outcome whereas others favor a **steric approach control**. Bicyclic systems such as camphor react primarily by steric influences which ultimately can be used to explain the ratio of the isomeric alcohols. If the camphor carbonyl is regarded as a flat

68

molecule, the H⁻ ion can add to the top or the bottom face of the carbonyl. However, not equally in approach. If one examines the camphor molecule the attack of the hydride from the bottom side, ***endo*-approach**, is easier than from the top, ***exo*-approach**. Why? You should comment in your report why this is and relate this rationale in your report with regards to product ratios. In other words, explain clearly why isoborneol, will predominate but not be the exclusive product in the final reaction mixture.

III) Experimental Procedure

Re-weigh the 10 or 25 mL Erlenmeyer flask containing the camphor from Experiment # 3. Determine the exact weight of the camphor. If you have less than 0.1 g, obtain more from the stockroom so you have at least that amount.

Add 0.5 mL of methanol to the camphor and swirl until the camphor dissolves. *Exert extreme care in handling sodium borohydride, it reacts violently if it comes in contact with water, and thus releasing a gas which is flammable.* In portions, cautiously and slowly add 0.060 g of sodium borohydride to the methanol solution. If the additions appear violent and the flask temperature elevates above room temperature, place the flask in an ice bath. After all the borohydride is added, heat the contents on a steam bath for ~5 minutes.

After heating, allow the reaction to cool to room temperature, and carefully add 4 mL of ice H₂O. Collect the white solid by vacuum filtration using a Hirsch funnel and allow to dry several minutes with suction applied. Transfer the solid to a 25 mL Erlenmeyer flask, add 5 mL of diethyl ether to dissolve the product, and add anhydrous sodium sulfate to dry the reaction mixture.

Remove the ether solution using a filter pipet, and place it into another small pre-weighed, clean filter flask. Add 1 mL of diethyl ether to the flask containing the drying agent to recover more of the product. Swirl the flask, filter the drying agent, and combine the diethyl ether layers. Evaporate the solvent under *vacuum* using an aspirator until an off-white solid results. Re-weigh the product and calculate the percent yield. Obtain the IR spectrum of the product (thin-film), and determine if you were successful in reducing camphor.

IV) ^1H NMR Analysis for the Isomeric Alcohol Percent

The approximate percentage of each of the isomeric alcohols in the borohydride reduction mixture can be determined by ^1H NMR. The hydrogen on the carbon bearing the hydroxyl group appears at approximately 4.0 ppm for borneol and 3.6 ppm for isoborneol. One can obtain the product ratio by integrating these peaks in the NMR spectrum obtained after reduction. A sample copy of this spectrum is provided. Determine the percentages of isoborneol and borneol. Comment on the percentages in your report and explain clearly if this result is what you expected and why.

V) Post-Lab Report:

Discuss the following in your Post-Lab report.

- Reductions in organic chemistry, general trends, and other reducing agents that can perform the aforementioned transformation above.
- A discussion of stereochemistry. diastereomers, enantiomers, etc.
- Include the mechanism of the reaction for the formation of the alcohols starting from camphor.
- Discuss important side reactions that can occur in this experiment.
- Clearly rationalize the percentages of the isomeric alcohol mixture in the ^1H NMR spectrum. Use theory to explain these results.
- Discuss if the reduction was successful and how you determined this.

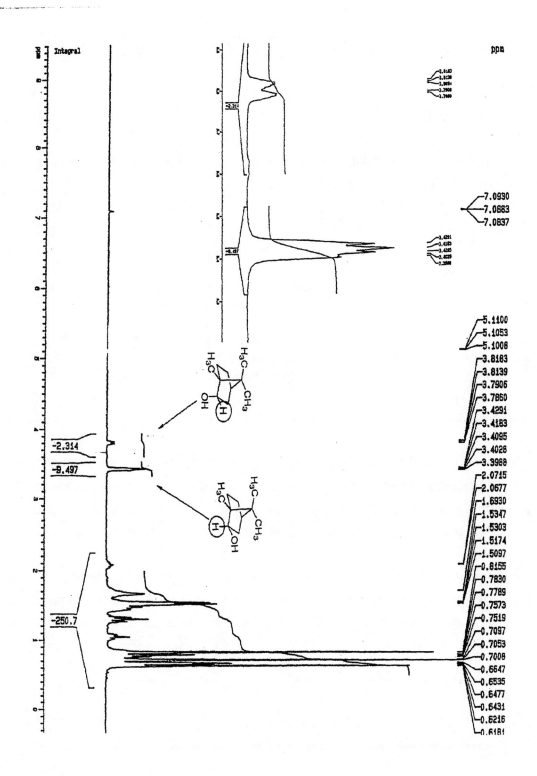

Experiment 4: Esterification-Synthesis of Methyl Benzoate

I) Aim of the Experiment

The purpose of this experiment is to synthesize methyl benzoate from benzoic acid and methanol by a Fischer esterification.

Methyl benzoate
bp 198-199 °C

II) Introduction

The ester group (RCO_2R') is an important functional group that can be synthesized by a variety of unique ways. Low molecular weight esters have very pleasant smelling odors, constituting the major components of the flavor and odor of a number of fruits and flowers. Esters are very often used as artificial flavoring in the food industry and also as fragrances.

Esters can be prepared by many different synthetic methods, but the two most common are **Fischer esterification** of a carboxylic acid with an alcohol in the presence of an acid catalyst, and the condensation of an acid chloride with an alcohol or alkoxide anion.

Because the reaction is readily reversible, (an equilibrium reaction), we must consider the magnitude or value of the equilibrium constant (K). By taking this value into

$$K = \frac{(Ester)\,(H_2O)}{(Acid)\,(Alcohol)}$$

account one may be able to modify the stoichiometric mixture of one of the starting materials, thus driving the equilibrium to the right, yielding the maximal amount of product. The position of the equilibrium can be shifted by adding more of the acid or of the alcohol, by **Le Chatelier's principle**, to yield the ester in high abundance. In our case, the alcohol is cheaper, and will be used as the reagent in excess. Another technique is available for manipulating the equilibrium in favor of making more ester. Removal of a product, such as water by azeotropic distillation also works reasonably well. To do this, one must use a **Dean-Starke apparatus**.

You should write a step-by-step mechanism in your lab report for the preparation of methyl benzoate from the corresponding starting material.

III) Experimental Procedure

Into a 10 mL conical vial, place 2 g of benzoic acid and 5.0 mL of methanol. Cool the mixture in an ice bath and add 0.6 mL of concentrated sulfuric acid. *Be careful when handling sulfuric acid, which can cause severe burns.* Swirl the vial to mix the components. Add a boiling stone and assemble a reflux apparatus using a water-cooled condenser.

Using a hot plate and a sand bath, bring the mixture to a boil and reflux the mixture for 1 hour. Remove the heated sand bath and allow the apparatus to cool to room temperature. Decant the solution into a small separatory funnel containing 10 mL of water, and rinse the vial with 10 mL of diethyl ether. Add this ether to the separatory funnel, shake thoroughly, and drain off the water layer (bottom), which will contain sulfuric acid and excess methanol. Wash the ether layer in the separatory funnel with 6 mL of water followed by 6 mL of 0.5 M sodium bicarbonate to remove unreacted carboxylic acid. Again shake, with frequent venting to release pressure by inverting the separatory funnel and opening the stopcock. Point this away from yourself and others. Repeat bicarbonate washings until the water layer is basic to pH paper, and no more gas evolution is evident. Drain off the bicarbonate layer into a small 50 mL beaker. Wash the ether layer with a few milliliters of saturated sodium chloride solution and dry the solution over anhydrous calcium chloride pellets in a 50 mL Erlenmeyer flask. Add sufficient calcium chloride pellets until they no longer clump together. After 10 minutes, decant the dry ether solution into a 125 mL vacuum flask. Add 3-4 mL of fresh ether to rinse the drying agent, and transfer to the flask. Cap the flask using a adaptor, and evaporate the solvent using an aspirator. Be sure a trap is used. The boiling point of diethyl ether is quite low, so the solvent should evaporate quickly. Upon evaporation of the solvent, you will be left with an oil, which you will purify, by distillation. Carefully, transfer the product using a pipet to a 5 mL vial. Add a boiling stone and assemble the distillation by attaching the Hickman still equipped with an air condenser. Place the apparatus in a sand bath and heat to a boil. The boiling point of the ester is very high (199 °C), so collect the material boiling above 190 °C. Use aluminum foil for insulation if necessary. Transfer the distillate to a pre-weighed conical vial using a pipet. Weigh the product, calculate percent yield, and take the IR spectrum of the pure product. Save the product for the next laboratory experiment.

IV) Post-Lab Report

In your Post-Lab report clearly discuss the following topics.

- Fischer Esterification: conditions, etc.
- Contrast kinetics versus equilibrium as applied to this reaction.
- Le Chatlier's principle as applied to this reaction, and ways one may manipulate the equilibrium to produce more ester in this synthesis.
- Include other general synthetic methods for the preparation of esters.
- A detailed mechanism for the production of methyl benzoate from the corresponding starting materials in the synthesis.
- Pertinent side reactions that can occur in this experiment.
- In the discussion section of your report, use the boiling point data and the IR spectrum to determine if methyl benzoate was indeed synthesized. Interpret your IR carefully, and compare your spectrum to the literature spectrum shown below. If the product is contaminated with a starting material, discuss what the contamination is, and how one may make alterations to the experimental procedure in order to obtain purer product.
- Below is the ^{1}H NMR spectrum of the product. Interpret the NMR carefully and include assignments made in your report.

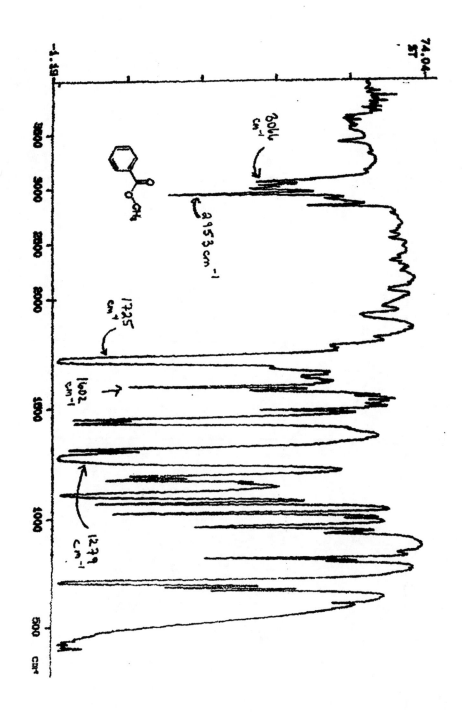

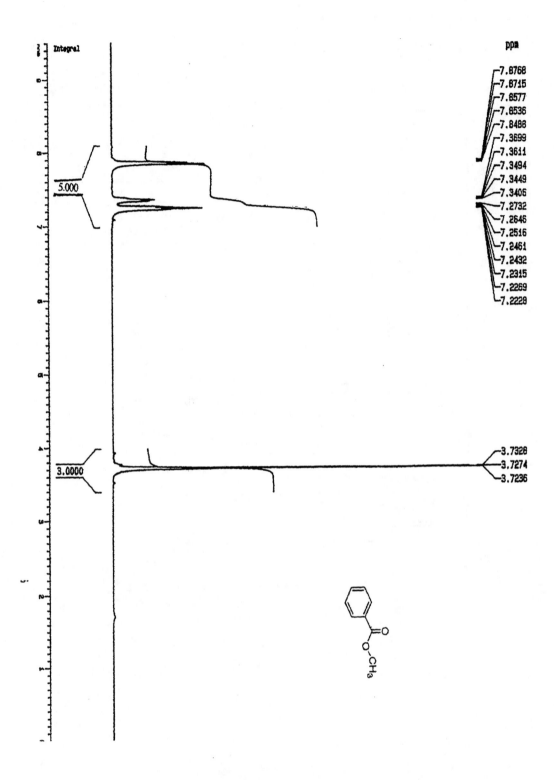

Experiment 5: Nitration of Methyl Benzoate

I) Aim of the Experiment

In this experiment, you will nitrate methyl benzoate to prepare methyl 3-nitrobenzoate.

Methyl benzoate $\xrightarrow[\substack{H_2SO_4 \\ "NO_2^{\oplus}"}]{HNO_3}$ Methyl 3-nitrobenzoate
mp 78 °C

II) Introduction

The nitration reaction described in this experiment follows an example of a classical **electrophilic aromatic substitution reaction**. Here, a proton on the aromatic ring is replaced by a nitro group.

Nitric acid reacts with the stronger acid, sulfuric acid, via an acid base reaction to give rise to the **nitronium ion** (NO_2^+) by the following equation.

$$HNO_3 + 2\ H_2SO_4 \rightleftharpoons NO_2^{\oplus} + 2\ HSO_4^{\ominus} + H_3O^{\oplus}$$

The nitronium cation serves as an electrophile (El^+) and attacks the electron rich benzene ring of methyl benzoate, with substitution of a proton.

The solvent, believe it or not, for this reaction is sulfuric acid and it protonates methyl benzoate. The nitronium ion then reacts quickly with this intermediate at a **meta** position, where the electron density is the highest due to resonance. You should convince yourself of this by drawing a proper reaction mechanism and include all necessary resonance

77

forms in the mechanism, and clearly illustrate the product formed. Since the nitro group is **deactivating**, the nitration usually stops at the mono-substituted product, however, exceptions are known when other groups are present. Note that the ester group serves as a **meta director** and deactivates the benzene ring.

III) Experimental Procedure

To a medium sized test tube, add 0.3 g of methyl benzoate from Experiment # 5 and 0.6 mL of concentrated sulfuric acid. If you do not have the sufficient amount of methyl benzoate, obtain the difference from the stock room. Flick the tube to mix and cool the tube in ice to 0 °C. Dropwise, add using a pipet, a mixture of 0.2 mL of concentrated sulfuric acid and 0.2 mL of concentrated nitric acid. *Use care in handling concentrated nitric and sulfuric acid.*

Keep the reaction mixture in ice, and using a stirring rod, mix the acid solution well, while taking care to allow the mixture not to rise above 15 °C as judged by touching the reaction tube.

After all the nitric acid has been added, warm the mixture to room temperature and after 15 minutes, pour it onto 3 g of cracked ice in a 50 mL beaker. Isolate the solid by vacuum filtration using a Hirsch funnel. Wash the product with cold H_2O and then with 0.5 mL of *ice* cold methanol. If the methanol is not ice-cold, you will lose product.

Transfer the solid to another test tube and recrystallize the product from an equal weight of methanol or alternatively dissolve the sample in a slightly larger quantity of methanol and add water dropwise to make the hot solution saturated with product. Slowly cool the product, which will give rise to the production of large crystals. Filter the product, record the mass of the product and calculate the percent yield. Obtain the melting point and compare it to the literature value.

IV) Post-lab Report

In you Post-Lab report clearly discuss the following points.

- Electrophilic aromatic substitution, theory, conditions, examples.
- List of activating and deactivating groups.
- List of *ortho, para* directors and *meta* directors.

- Mechanism of this reaction. Include important resonance structures which show why the product forms.
- Side reactions that can occur in this experiment.
- Obtain and attach the literature IR spectrum of the product and interpret carefully. Also, interpret the ^{1}H NMR of the product shown below.
- Comment on if you had synthesized the correct product by interpreting the melting point data.

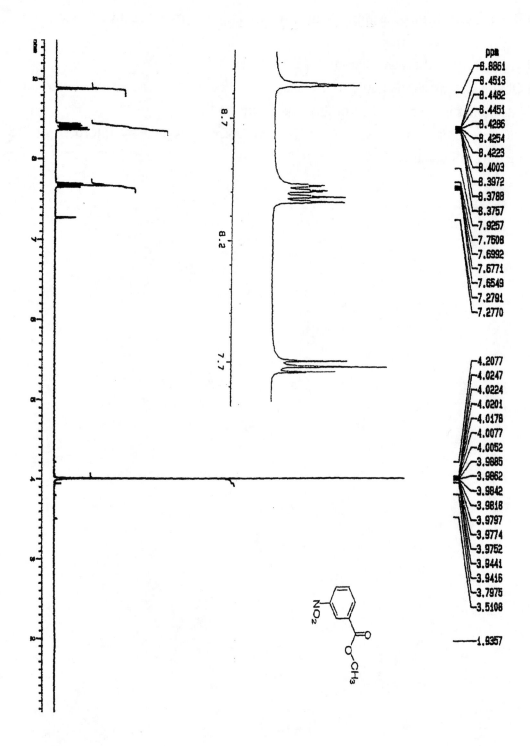

ppm
8.8861
8.4513
8.4482
8.4451
8.4286
8.4254
8.4223
8.4003
8.3972
8.3788
8.3757
7.9257
7.7508
7.6992
7.6771
7.6549
7.2791
7.2770

4.2077
4.0247
4.0224
4.0201
4.0178
4.0077
4.0052
3.9885
3.9862
3.9842
3.9818
3.9797
3.9774
3.9752
3.9441
3.9416
3.7975
3.5106

1.9357

Experiment 6: Friedel-Crafts Acylation of Ferrocene

I) Aim of the Experiment

The purpose of this experiment is to acylate the organometallic compound, ferrocene, by a Friedel-Crafts acylation and to purify it by column chromatography.

Ferrocene   Acetic Anhydride   Acetyl Ferrocene   Acetic Acid

mp 173 °C   mp 85-86 °C

II) Introduction

The **Friedel-Crafts acylation** of ferrocene gives rise to the formation of acetyl ferrocene by reacting it with acetic anhydride in the presence of an acid catalyst, phosphoric acid (H_3PO_4). Typically, Lewis acids have been traditionally used, such as aluminum chloride, however ferrocene can be acylated under mild conditions with the use of phosphoric acid. With the use of this acid, the **acylium cation** is generated (the electrophile), by protonation of acetic anhydride and loss of acetic acid.

Acylium cation
(electrophile)

The acylium cation then attacks the cyclopentadienyl ring of ferrocene, resulting in substitution of the acetyl group for a ring proton. You should draw a reasonable mechanism in your report for the acylation of ferrocene.

Acetyl ferrocene and ferrocene are both highly colored compounds and are easily separable by column chromatography.

III) Experimental Procedure

To a small test tube, add 93 mg of dry ferrocene, 0.35 mL of acetic anhydride, and 0.1 mL phosphoric acid (*handle acetic anhydride and phosphoric acid in the hood with care*). Cap the tube with a rubber septum, place a syringe needle through the top, and dissolve the ferrocene by heating the mixture with agitation on a steam bath using a pair of test tube holders. Heat the mixture ten minutes longer, and allow it to cool to room temperature and then place the test tube in an ice bath.

Add 0.5 mL of ice water dropwise with mixing to the solution, followed by dropwise addition of 3 M NaOH until the mixture is neutral (test with pH paper). Avoid adding excess base. Collect the product by vacuum filtration using a Hirsch funnel and wash the product thoroughly with cold water. Press the product between two pieces of filter paper and remove a few milligrams for a melting point. Purify the remainder by column chromatography.

Column Chromatography

Obtain a Pasteur pipet from the stockroom. *Carefully,* snap the tip as demonstrated by your instructor. Prepare a microscale column by placing a small plug of glass wool down into the stem using a thin stirring rod or wooden stick. Place the pipet through a one-hole rubber stopper and clamp the pipet vertically. Place a small beaker beneath it, and add ~500 mg of alumina to the column. Continue adding alumina until the column is about 2/3 full. Add a small layer of sand on the top and fill the column with hexanes and allow the solvent to drip out of the pipet into the beaker. Make sure the column is packed tight and no air bubbles are caught within the packing material. If air bubbles are present, consult your instructor. Allow the hexanes level to reach the top of the sand and place a labeled 10 mL Erlenmeyer flask (Fraction #1) underneath the column.

Dissolve your product in a small amount of hexanes and using a pipet, transfer to the column. Use an additional small amount more hexanes to complete the transfer. When all of the crude product is transferred to the column, allow the solvent level to run to bed level and begin eluting with hexanes. As you elute, various colorful bands will be noticed, but only one will move more quickly down the column. This yellow-colored band is ferrocene. Collect this band into a 10 mL flask. If you notice any crystalline material beginning to form on the pipet, wash them down into the flask with one or two drops of diethyl ether. Without allowing the column to run dry, add a 50:50 mixture of hexanes-diethyl ether and next elute the acetyl ferrocene. This band will be orange-colored. Collect this band into another 10 mL flask (label as fraction #2). Record all observations in your notebook.

TLC these two solutions and compare them against the stock solution of ferrocene supplied. Develop the plate in a TLC chamber containing a mixture of 30:1 toluene:absolute ethanol supplied. Record all observations in your notebook.

Isolate each product by evaporating the solvent by placing each solution in a separate, pre-weighed small filter flask. Cap the flask with a rubber stopper and attach the side arm to the aspirator. Using the warmth from your hand as a heat source, remove the solvent under vacuum while swirling.

Isolate the products, dry them, determine their weights, and record their melting points. Compare the physical data with the literature values.

IV) Post-Lab Report

In your Post-Lab write-up discuss the following points.

• Friedel-Crafts Alkylation: conditions, examples, etc.
• Friedel-Crafts Acylation: conditions, examples, etc.
• Mechanism of this reaction using the starting materials in this synthesis.
• Side products that can be generated in this experiment.
• Other acylation methods (*i.e.*, other catalysts) and examples.
• Benefits and limitations to this reaction.
• Interpret the melting point data and compare them to the literature values. Also, comment if the reaction, as well as the purification, was successful using the TLC data.
• Below is the ^{1}H NMR for acetylferrocene. Interpret the spectrum carefully.

ppm

—7.2781

—4.7960
—4.5278
—4.4722
—4.2864
—4.2299

—2.4119
—2.3626

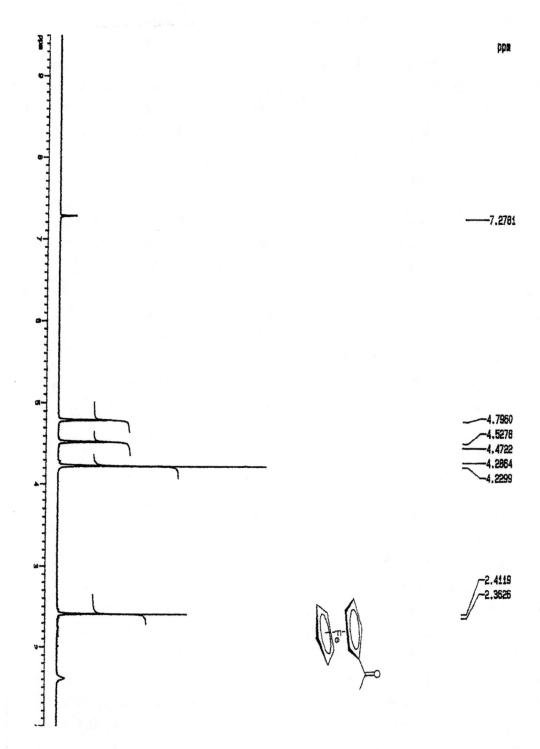

Experiment 7: Preparation of a 2,4-Dinitro-Phenylhydrazone Derivative of an Unknown Aldehyde or Ketone

I) Aim of the Experiment

In this experiment, you will prepare a 2,4-dinitrophenylhydrazone derivative of an unknown aldehyde or ketone, and identify the unknown by its melting point.

II) Introduction

Carbonyl groups play a central role in organic chemistry with regards to reactivity. The electronegative oxygen atom polarizes the carbon-oxygen bond, rendering the carbon electron-deficient and hence subject to nucleophilic addition.

Amines add to the carbonyl group readily to give compounds known as **imines** (R_2-C=N), upon loss of water. These imines are often solids and can be very useful for the characterization of an unknown aldehyde or ketone.

Although numerous derivatives are known, the 2,4-dinitrophenylhydrazone will be the derivative of choice in this lab, because it gives nice crystalline compounds with well-defined melting points. These melting points can be correlated with previously prepared derivatives in the literature to determine the unknown you possess.

III) Experimental Procedure

In this experiment, you should run a known aldehyde or ketone along side of your unknown to familiarize yourself with what to expect.

Obtain an unknown from your instructor. Record the number in your notebook, and any necessary physical data such as color, odor and etc.

In a clean small test tube, dissolve 100 mg (or if a liquid ~3 drops) of the unknown carbonyl compound in 2 mL of ethanol and add 3 mL of 2,4-dinitrophenylhydrazine reagent. *Be careful when handling this reagent, it is an irritant and stains the skin. This reagent also contains sulfuric acid, which is corrosive and can cause severe burns.*

A large mass of crystals usually will form immediately, however heating may be necessary to produce the derivative. Allow the mixture to stand at room temperature for 20 minutes and collect the product by suction filtration using a Hirsch funnel. Wash the crystals three times with 1 mL of cold ethanol at each washing. It is extremely important to wash these crystals thoroughly to remove all the sulfuric acid (litmus). Any remaining sulfuric acid that may adhere to the crystals will decompose the product when you take the melting point, causing a lower and broadened melting point range.

Determine the melting point. If recrystallization proves to be necessary, use ethanol as the solvent. Compare your melting point with the tabulated values and determine your unknown identity.

IV) Post-Lab Report

In your Post-Lab report discuss the following.

- Discuss imine formation, conditions, etc.
- Purpose of a derivative.
- Include other derivatives of aldehydes and ketones: Hydrazone, semicarbazone, oxime, and phenylhydrazone.
- Mechanism of the reaction using your unknown as the starting material.
- Side reactions that can occur in this experiment.
- Clearly discuss how you identified the unknown using the melting point data. Comment on purity and how close your value is to the literature.

Experiment 8: Grignard Synthesis of Triphenylmethanol

I) Aim of the Experiment

In this experiment, you will synthesize the tertiary alcohol, triphenylmethanol, from *in situ* generated phenylmagnesium bromide and benzophenone.

Bromobenzene → Phenyl Magnesium Bromide (a Grignard Reagent) → Triphenylmethanol mp 164 °C

II) Introduction

The Grignard reagent, an organomagnesium reagent, as generally understood is an orgnomagnesium-halide-ether complex that is formed by the action of magnesium metal with an organic halide in an anhydrous solvent such as diethyl ether. The structure of the organometallic species in solution is rather complex and not well understood, however, the species are thought to form aggregates in solution.

The **Grignard reagent** is, however, well known to behave as both a strong base and a great nucleophile. Since it acts as a strong base, all reactants and apparatus must be completely dry (no acidic protons *i.e.* H_2O) or the reaction will not proceed. If proper precautions are taken, the reaction will proceed smoothly. These reagents are extremely powerful on synthetic scale for carbon-carbon bond formation.

This reagent will be converted to a tertiary alcohol upon reaction with a ketone, benzophenone. The alkyl portion of the Grignard reagent behaves as a **carbanion** (R_3C^-) which readily attacks the electrophilic carbon atom of the carbonyl.

You should propose an acceptable mechanism for the formation of triphenyl methanol starting from the appropriate starting materials in your report.

III) Experimental Procedure

It is important to work efficiently in this experiment, time will be of essence. All glassware used in this reaction must be scrupulously dry!! Flame dry all pieces of glassware, then place the glassware in an oven at 110 °C until ready to use. Do not heat plastic parts.

A. Preparation of the Grignard Reagent: Phenylmagnesium Bromide

Flame dry the following items from your lab kit: two 3 mL, two 5 mL conical vials, a Claisen adapter, a small beaker, a drying tube containing anhydrous calcium chloride and a calibrated Pasteur pipet (0.5 mL and 1.0 mL calibration marks) right before using each item. Place these items in an oven at 110 °C until ready for use. Do not place plasticware or plastic syringes in the oven as they may melt. There should be no visible signs of water in the apparatus.

Weigh out .037 g of magnesium metal turnings into a small dry beaker. Place the magnesium into a dry 5 mL conical vial, and fit the vial with a Claisen head, a calcium chloride drying tube containing calcium chloride, and a rubber septum.

Add 4 mL of **anhydrous** diethyl ether into a capped **dry** 5 mL conical vial. *Caution: Since diethyl ether is flammable and a narcotic, please extinguish all flames before its use and do not breathe its vapor.* During the experiment, remove the ether from the vial using a syringe by piercing the rubber adapter.

Place 0.17 mL of bromobenzene into a pre-weighed 3 mL conical vial and record its weight in your notebook. Add 1 mL of anhydrous diethyl ether to the vial and dissolve the bromobenzene. Draw this solution into a syringe and insert the needle through the septum on the apparatus. Add 0.2 mL of the prepared bromobenzene solution to the magnesium in the vial. Position the apparatus just above a sand bath made by filling a heating mantle well with sand, which is then plugged into a variac. Agitate and swirl the mixture. However, avoid throwing the magnesium onto the wall of the vial. Bubbles should appear from the surface of the magnesium, which designates the reaction is beginning. It will probably be necessary to warm the mixture by heating in a sand bath of about 60 °C (use a thermometer) to initiate the reaction. Since diethyl ether has a low boiling point, it may be sufficient to just heat the vial above the warm sand bath. If the reaction does not begin when heated, remove the syringe and the septum, and use a **dry** glass-stirring rod to gently crush the magnesium (Careful not to break glassware!). If this does not seem to initiate the reaction, add a crystal of solid iodine to the vial. Observe. If nothing still occurs at this point you may wish to use a small amount of Grignard reagent that has already been generated successfully by another student. Add it to the mixture in the vial.

Upon initiation of the reaction, you should begin to observe a solution that appears brownish gray and cloudy in appearance. At this point, add the rest of the bromobenzene solution over 5 minutes. It may be necessary to continually warm during the addition, however, if during the addition the reaction refluxes too vigorously, slow the addition of the reagent (bromobenzene). However, it is *extremely important you warm the mixture if the reflux is too slow or stops.* Upon adding the halide, you should see the magnesium begin to dissolve. After all the bromobenzene solution is added, add 0.5 mL of anhydrous diethyl ether to the vial that contained the original bromobenzene solution and add it to the reaction mixture using the same syringe. If you have foreseen a loss of diethyl ether in the reaction mixture due to vigorous reflux, add more. After 45 minutes from the first addition of the bromobenzene, all of the magnesium metal should have reacted (dissolved).

B. Synthesis of Triphenylmethanol

Remove the sand bath and allow the vial to cool to room temperature. During this time period, prepare a solution of 0.27 g of benzophenone in 0.5 mL of anhydrous diethyl ether in a 3 mL conical vial. Cap the vial. When your vial is cooled from part A, using a syringe, rapidly add the benzophenone solution to the Grignard reagent. Be careful that the solution does not boil through. Upon adding all the benzophenone, cool the mixture to room temperature at which point the solution should turn to red and solidify. Remove the syringe and septum and stir the mixture using a clean dry spatula. Rinse the empty vial containing the benzophenone with 0.2 mL of diethyl ether and add this to the red mixture. Cap the reception vial and occasionally swirl it. The product should be fully formed within 20 minutes.

Add dropwise 2 mL of 6 M hydrochloric acid to neutralize the reaction mixture. *Be careful, 6 M HCl can cause severe burns!* You should think about the purpose of adding HCl at this point to the reaction mixture.

You should now see 2 phases in the vial. The organic layer (top) should contain the triphenylmethanol and the bottom HCl layer should contain the inorganic products.

You may have to use a spatula to break up any solid that forms during the addition of the HCl. Cap the vial and shake to dissolve the solid with venting. Add 1 mL of diethyl ether, and if necessary more HCl to dissolve any solid that remains. *At this point make sure you have two distinct layers and no solid.* Draw off the aqueous layer (bottom) using a pipet and save it in another conical vial. Extract this with 0.5 mL of diethyl ether using a pipet. Remove the aqueous layer and discard. Using a clean pipet, combine the 2 organic layers together and dry using anhydrous sodium sulfate.

Transfer the dried ether solution to a small filter flask, and rinse the drying agent with more diethyl ether. Add the washings to the flask and evaporate the solvent under vacuum using an aspirator.

Upon evaporation, you should be left with a brownish oil or a mushy colored solid mixed containing an oil. This contains your product and an impurity. Think about what the impurity is.

Add 1 mL of petroleum ether (bp 30-60 °C) to the flask, heat the mixture on a steam bath and swirl. Cool the mixture to room temperature. Collect triphenylmethanol by vacuum filtration using a Hirsch funnel and rinse with small portions of cold petroleum ether.

Dry the solid (press between two pieces of filter paper), weigh, and calculate the percent yield of the crude triphenylmethanol.

Transfer the crude product to a test tube and recrystallize from hot isopropyl alcohol. If insoluble impurities remain, consult your instructor. Set the test tube aside and allow to cool. Collect and dry crystals, obtain its weight and report its melting point. Compare its melting point with the literature value.

IV) Post-Lab Report

Discuss the following points in your Post-Lab report.

- Grignard reaction: theory, conditions, synthetic utility, etc.
- Restrictions and limitations to the reaction.
- Mechanism of the reaction starting from generation of the Grignard reagent.
- Reactions of Grignard reagents, examples, etc.
- Side reactions which can occur under these conditions.
- Other related organometallic reagents (*i.e.* organolithium reagents).
- Discuss if triphenylmethanol was successfully formed by interpreting the melting point data. If the product was not triphenylmethanol, discuss the identity of the product, its purity, and what you think had occurred. Offer solutions to correct the problem.

• Obtain the literature IR spectrum of tripheylmethanol, and interpret carefully. Also, shown below is the ^{1}H NMR of the product, make the appropriate assignments.

ppm

7.5370
7.3609
7.3586
7.3564
7.3530
7.3501
7.3385
7.3244
7.3140
7.3120
7.3052
7.3000
7.2953
7.2926
7.2791
7.2773
7.0923

15.000

1.031

2.8223

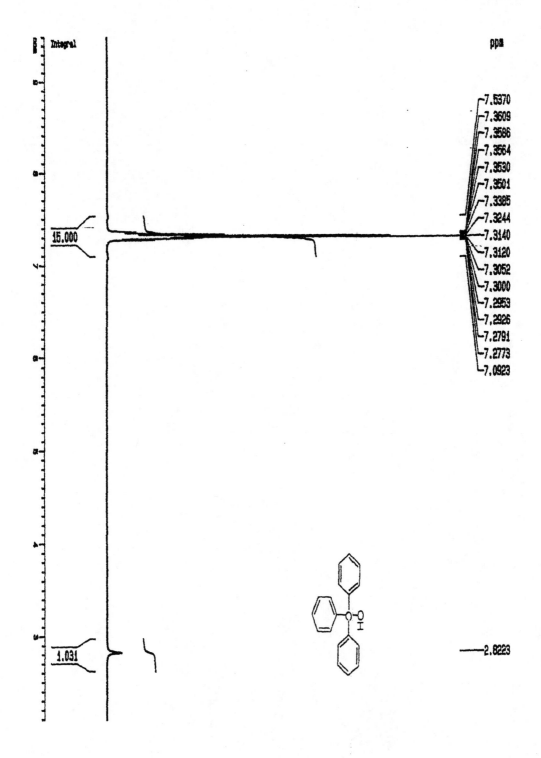

Experiment 9: Wittig Reaction-Synthesis of *trans*-9-(2-phenylethenyl) Anthracene

I) Aim of the Experiment

The purpose of this experiment is to synthesize *trans*-9-(2-phenylethenyl) anthracene from benzyltriphenylphosphonium chloride and 9-anthraldehyde via a Wittig reaction.

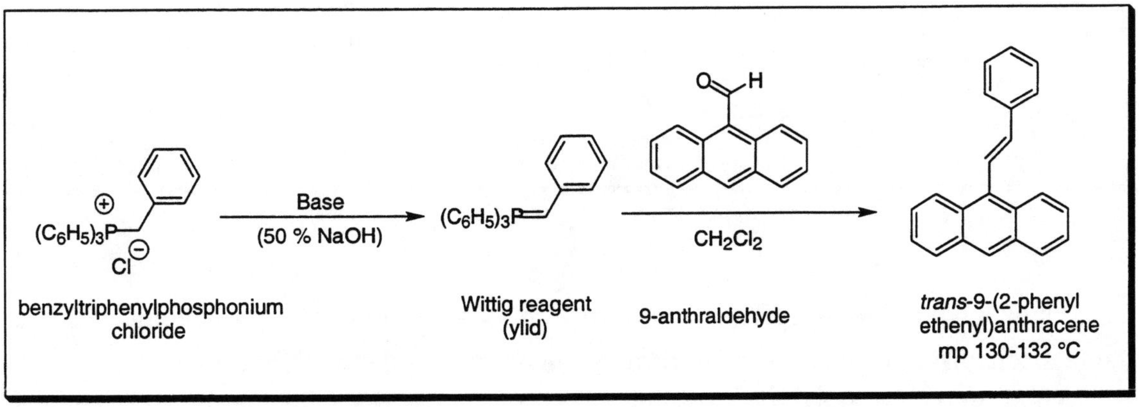

benzyltriphenylphosphonium chloride → Base (50 % NaOH) → Wittig reagent (ylid) + 9-anthraldehyde → CH$_2$Cl$_2$ → *trans*-9-(2-phenyl ethenyl)anthracene mp 130-132 °C

II) Introduction

The **Wittig** reaction is commonly used to convert a carbonyl group, C=O , into an alkene, C=C. The reaction involves the formation of a phosphorus **ylid** obtained by treatment of a phosphonium salt with a strong base. Phosphorous ylids are stable (due to resonance), highly reactive species, that are generally not isolatable, and are treated with carbonyl compounds as seen below.

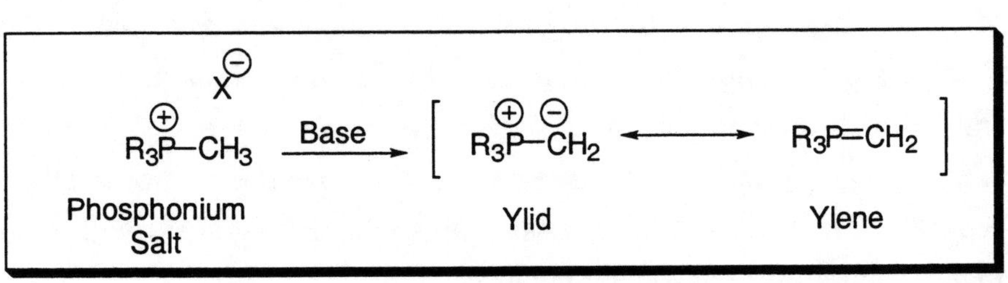

Phosphonium Salt → Base → [Ylid ↔ Ylene]

93

Upon generation of the ylid, the nucleophilic ylid carbon adds to the carbonyl group to give an intermediate known as **betaine**, followed by elimination of phosphine oxide. The elimination is presumed to occur after formation of a four-membered ring known as an **oxaphosphetane**. However, experimental evidence has shown the reaction might proceed directly through the oxaphosphetane intermediate.

Upon alkaline hydrolysis, the olefin product is produced. You should write a suitable mechanism in your report for forming the product in the reaction.

Since ylids are generally prepared by treatment of the phosphonium salt with a strong base to generate the desired ylid, all you need to do in this experiment is add a suitable solvent and the base sodium hydroxide.

III)   *Experimental Procedure*

To a 5 mL conical vial, add a spin vane, 200 mg of benzyltriphenylphosphonium chloride, 115 mg of 9-anthraldehyde, and add 0.6 mL of dichloromethane. Place the vial on a stir plate in the hood, and with rapid stirring, add 0.3 mL of 50 % NaOH solution dropwise using a Pasteur pipet. Stir the reaction mixture for 30 minutes. After 30 minutes, add 1.5 mL of dichloromethane and 1.5 mL of water. Cap the vial, and shake. Remove the organic layer using a pipet, and place it in a test tube. Extract the aqueous layer with an additional 1 mL of dichloromethane and combine the organic layers. Dry the combined dichloromethane layers with calcium chloride pellets. Remove the dichloromethane using a pipet and place it in a clean 125 mL filter flask. Rinse the drying agent with more solvent (dichloromethane) and remove the solvent under vacuum.

To the solid remaining in the flask, add 3 mL of 1-propanol and heat using a hot plate. Transfer the hot solution to a 50 mL Erlenmeyer flask and allow to crystallize. After cooling to room temperature, cool in an ice bath and collect the product by vacuum filtration using a Hirsch funnel. The by-product, triphenylphosphine oxide will remain in the 1-propanol solution.

Weigh and calculate the percent yield. Determine the melting point and compare it to the literature value.

IV) *Post-Lab Report*

Clearly discuss the following points in your Post-lab report.

- Wittig reaction: theory, conditions, examples, etc.
- Mechanism of the reaction in this experiment.
- Side reactions that occur.
- Related reactions to the Wittig reaction to make olefins.
- Discuss the stereoselectivity of this reaction. Why is the *trans* isomer only observed and not the *cis* ? Relate your explanation to kinetic vs. thermodynamic product.
- Compare your experimental melting point to the literature. Comment on identity and purity.

Experiment 10: Synthesis of Dibenzalacetone
by the Aldol Condensation

I) Aim of the Experiment

In this experiment, you will synthesize dibenzalacetone from benzaldehyde and acetone by the aldol condensation.

II) Introduction

The reaction of an aldehyde with a ketone using sodium hydroxide as a base is an example of a mixed **aldol condensation**, commonly known as the **Claisen-Schmidt reaction**.

The aldol condensation reaction is a fundamental reaction in organic synthesis in the formation of carbon-carbon bonds.

Dibenzalacetone is prepared by condensing one mole of acetone with 2 moles of benzaldehyde. The carbonyl group of the aldehyde is more reactive than the ketone, and upon deprotonation of the alpha carbon atom to give the anion of the ketone, it can perform a nucleophilic attack on the aldehyde, giving the β-hydroxy ketone, which spontaneously loses water to give the olefin. If another mole of aldehyde is present, or in this case with excess base, the reaction can occur again as before giving rise to the formation of the product, dibenzalacetone.

You should clearly illustrate in your report the detailed mechanism for the formation of dibenzalacetone, starting from benzaldehyde and acetone.

III) Experimental Procedure

Into a medium sized test tube, place 2 mL of 3 M NaOH solution. *Be careful not to get sodium hydroxide on your skin because it can cause burns.* To this solution, add 1.6 mL of 95% ethanol, 0.212 g of benzaldehyde, and 0.058 g of acetone. Cap the tube with a cork and shake the mixture vigorously. Benzaldehyde, which initially is insoluble, goes into solution, resulting in a pale yellow solution. After one minute or so, the solution will become cloudy and a yellow precipitate will form. Continually over a 30 minute time period, shake the tube occasionally, and if the product fails to crystallize, open the tube and scratch the inside walls with a glass stirring rod.

Remove the liquid from the test tube by using a pipet, firmly placed at the bottom of the tube. Be sure only to allow the liquid into the pipet, leaving the crystals behind. Add 3 mL of H_2O, cap the tube and shake vigorously. Remove the water as before and repeat twice more with 3 mL portions of H_2O. After the final washing, add 3 mL of water to the tube and collect the yellow solid by vacuum filtration using a Hirsch funnel. Remove and transfer as much crystals as possible. Dry the crude dibenzalacetone by squeezing the product between two pieces of filter paper. Recrystallize the dibenzalacetone from a 70:30 ethanol-H_2O mixture. Insert a boiling stick to promote boiling. Remove the test tube from the steam bath and allow to cool to room temperature.

If the product oils out, separates as an oil and not as a solid, consult your instructor. Cool the test tube in an ice bath for 10 minutes and collect the product as before by vacuum filtration. Wash the crystals with 0.5 mL of *ICE COLD* 70% ethanol.

Place the solid in a pre-weighed small filter flask, cap the flask with a rubber stopper, and remove traces of solvent under vacuum by attaching it to an aspirator. Scrape the solid out of the flask, and press it between two pieces of filter paper to further dry the crystals.

Determine the weight of the pure dibenzalacetone, and obtain its melting point. Compare the experimental melting point to the literature, and calculate its percent yield.

IV) Post-Lab Report

Include the following in your Post-Lab report.

- Discussion of the Aldol condensation, enolates, examples, synthetic utility.
- Mechanism of the reaction using the starting materials in this synthesis.

- Side reactions that can occur in this experiment.
- Related reactions to the aldol condensation.
- Limitations to this reaction.
- Comparison of the experimental melting point to the literature value.
- Obtain the literature IR spectrum for dibenzalacetone and interpret the spectrum in your report. Also, shown below is the ^{1}H NMR of the product. Make the appropriate assignments.

Go on to experiment 11, set up the initial part, and leave the reaction in your drawer until the next lab period.

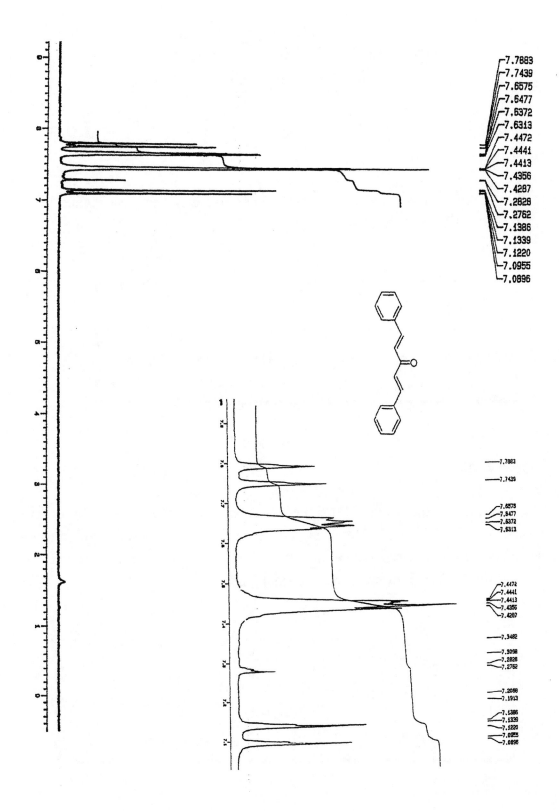

7.7883
7.7439
7.6575
7.6477
7.6372
7.6313
7.4472
7.4441
7.4413
7.4356
7.4287
7.2828
7.2762
7.1386
7.1339
7.1220
7.0955
7.0896

7.7883
7.7439
7.6575
7.6477
7.6372
7.6313
7.4472
7.4441
7.4413
7.4356
7.4287
7.3482
7.3098
7.2828
7.2762
7.2069
7.1913
7.1386
7.1339
7.1220
7.0955
7.0896

Experiment 11: Enzymatic Reactions:
Enzymatic Reaction of a Ketone to a Chiral Alcohol

I) Aim of the Experiment

In this experiment, you will use the enzymes found in yeast to reduce Ethyl acetoacetate to (S)-(+)-Ethyl 3-hydroxybutanoate.

Ethyl acetoacetate   (S)-(+)-Ethyl 3-hydroxybutanoate

n_D^{20} 1.4210

II) Introduction

We have seen in experiment # 3 that the reduction of a ketone (camphor) will give rise to the synthesis of an alcohol. However, reduction of an achiral ketone with a usual laboratory reducing agent like $NaBH_4$ will not lead to a chiral alcohol. This is due to equal chances of attack on both sides of the planar carbonyl group.

In modern synthetic organic chemistry, it is often necessary to use optically pure starting materials to prepare a target molecule such as a drug in enantiomerically pure form.

If the reducing agent is chiral, it is possible to obtain the resulting chiral alcohol as optically pure. There are certain enzymes found in nature that perform this enantioselective reduction efficiently.

A large number of enzymes are present in yeast, however, only one reducing enzyme will carry out the reaction. The enzyme responsible for the conversion is the same as the one involved in the metabolism of D-glucose to ethanol.

Whenever a chiral product is obtained from an achiral starting material, chemical yields are not generally important. However, optical yields, such as enantomeric excess (ee), lets you know how stereoselective the reaction was. Review concepts of enantomeric excess and polarimetry from the chirality experiment in organic laboratory 1.

Typical reported enantiomeric excess for the enzymatic reduction of ethyl acetoacete has been reported by various authors. Reported ranges vary from 70-97%.

III) Experimental Procedure

A) Part I

To a 50 mL Erlenmeyer flask, dissolve 2.3 g of sucrose and add 15 mg of disodium hydrogen phosphate, 8.5 mL of warm (35 °C) tap water, and 0.5 g of dry yeast. Swirl the suspension thoroughly. After 15 minutes, add 150 mg of ethyl acetoacetate to the fermentation broth. Cover the yeast with foil, and store the flask in a warm place (30-35 °C), your lab drawer will suffice, until next lab period.

B) Part II

At the beginning of the next lab period, add 0.5 g of Celite® filtration aid, and remove the yeast cells by filtration using a Hirsch funnel. Wash the cells with 2 mL of water, then saturate the filtrate using sodium chloride to decrease the solubility of the product, this is called "salting out". Consult a handbook for the solubility of sodium chloride in water to decide approximately how much salt to add to your volume of solution.

Extract the solution five times with 2 mL portions of diethyl ether in a test tube. Shake will enough to efficiently mix the layers, but not too hard that an emulsion forms between the two layers.

Dry the organic layer using anhydrous sodium sulfate until the drying agent no longer clumps up. After 15 minutes, place the diethyl ether solution into a pre-weighed small filter flask. Cap the flask and evaporate the solvent under vacuum using an aspirator. Weigh the product.

TLC your residue (dissolve the residue in dichloromethane) and spot it against the starting material (ethyl acetoacetate). Measure the optical rotation and report % ee value. If time allows, obtain the IR spectrum of the product. Interpret the spectrum carefully.

IV) *Post-Lab Report*

Discuss the following concepts in your Post-Lab report.

- Enzymatic reactions, conditions, examples, as applied to this reaction, etc.
- Optical purity of the product, ee, etc.
- Side reactions.
- Mechanism.
- Possible problems and solutions in this reaction.